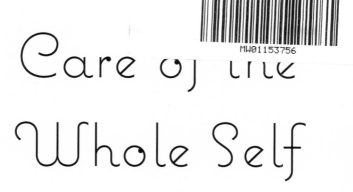

Care of the Whole Self

Yoga-Inspired Practices for Befriending the Self

Maryam Ovissi

This book is dedicated to those who lost their lives and to those who served on the frontlines of the COVID-19 global pandemic

May Peace surround ALL

Table of Contents

Foreword

Our collective experience of the global pandemic we're currently in is the perfect context for me to launch this labor of love, which I have been working on for more than three years. I decided on an early launch of this important resource—because this is the best moment I can think of to share powerful tools for the care of the whole self!

We are already living in stressful and difficult times, and something as major as a global pandemic can hijack our nervous systems in ways that make it hard for us to function, individually and collectively. Without tools that invite whole-self-care, we can find ourselves stumbling into the downward spiral and becoming not just overwhelmed, but traumatized.

In a recent blog, speaker and gift economy advocate Charles Eisenstein shares:

> *COVID-19 is like a rehab intervention that breaks the addictive hold of normality. To interrupt a habit is to make it visible; it is to turn it from a compulsion to a choice. When the crisis subsides, we might have occasion to ask whether we want to return to normal, or whether there might be something we've seen during this break in the routines that we want to bring into the future.*

In light of Eisenstein's sage words, I know that *Care of the Whole Self* can be a tool for you to stay tethered during this time so you can find your power of choice and enter a new way of being in alignment with yourself and our home, this beautiful and fragile planet.

To that end, I am offering this book. Please enjoy it, put it into practice, and share your feedback. Most importantly, explore and invite the curious child within you to choose to care for your whole self.

I have so many to thank on this journey. Gratitude to editor extraordinaire, Nirmala Nataraj, who lovingly and skillfully nudged me along. Gratitude to designer Bita Ghavami, who joined the team with enthusiasm and generously shared her talents as an artist and social media vizier to support the birth of this book. Many of you who will read these words will know you have impacted me with your presence, teachings, and lives. I thank you.

At the end of my yoga classes, I speak these words. May they resonate with you.

We bow to all of our teachers
In all of their forms
And to the greatest teacher
The great companion within
Namaha Namaste

Introduction

Having spent more than 20 years in the field of yoga and having clocked at least 20,000 teaching hours, I have developed the ability to observe how humans are motivated to take care of themselves. I wrote this book after 15 years of watching thousands of people deal with so many imbalances, knowing many of them could have been avoided with thoughtful whole-self-care practices. In this book, I want to offer you tools and teachings to inspire you to be deliberate and encouraged in your care of the whole self.

At the core of yoga is a whole-self-care methodology. Having a teacher is very important. Yet the teacher is only a guide. The practitioner is the one who is making the choice to practice, to be deliberate, and to stoke the fire of inspiration for themselves over time.

We have so much science accessible to us to explain why preventative practices make a difference. It's up to you as the practitioner to choose to utilize these tools. Yet why do so many of us continue to hijack our best intentions and refrain from making wise, informed decisions?

You might get an idea when you take a moment to look at a typical day for most of the clients I work with:

- Alarm goes off and shocks the nervous system into "awakeness"
- Wake-up rituals ensue and often include caffeine and not much movement or contemplation
- The commute to work, which usually includes traffic and frustration
- The workday plays out, entailing lots of sitting (again, not much movement), computer screens that strain the eyes and work overtime to impair the health of the brain and body, and organizational practices that might further a sense of disconnection and frustration
- The reverse commute, which spurs a combination of relief about the end of the work day and dread over what comes next (what to make for dinner, running random errands, helping other members of the household, etc.)
- The brain and body remain in a stimulated state, due to lack of rest and/or reflective inner work, moving on to other activities such as helping children with homework, working out, dinner, etc.
- Bedtime rituals might include mindless activities such as scrolling screens and binge-watching Netflix to try to quiet the nervous system (however, what's actually happening is that the body is fatigued but the nervous system isn't relaxed, so a person might fall asleep only to awaken a few hours later with a hyperactive mind)
- Sleep occurs but is often interrupted by insomnia
- The alarm goes off the next day and the cycle repeats

If you examine the layout of the day above, where is the rest and the pause of the day? The senses are constantly scanning and taking in information while the brain is ceaselessly processing, evaluating, and making decisions. This in itself is stressful, despite the interactions, conversations, and experiences that are sprinkled throughout the day. It's easy to understand why we tend to remain in a state of constant stress at all times.

I believe one of the ways to make that shift is through the diligent care of the *whole* self. The technology of yoga has always recognized the layers of the whole self. Yoga has taken different forms and shapes over the last 5,000 years, but it has always aspired to one thing. My teachers, the Mohans, call it *svastha*, a Sanskrit word that means "well-being." This well-being is not solely about the health of the body, the steadiness of the breath, or the peace of one's inner landscape. Svastha speaks to the well-being of the whole self. The necessity of each part to the whole is monumental and needs to be respected and consciously observed.

The ancient yoga sage Patanjali's eight limbs of yoga (*ashtanga*, not to be confused with the contemporary modality of yoga) offer a framework for all the self-care tools I share in this book. I refer to ashtanga as a technology system. I think of it as being similar to hardware. How it is brought to life is through the energy and intention of the practitioner, like the electricity that powers a computer. No matter how extraordinary your computer is, without energy, it is powerless. Think about it—what affects the electrical system of our homes? The quality of the wires, the source of electricity, the grid from which it pulls, and how the energy is used. Similarly, what affects our vitality in our body? Our DNA/genes, our nutrition, our environment, and how we use our energy.

In these times, which are accelerated, data-driven, and fast, we need to practice now more than ever the skill of lingering, pausing, and just sitting and being with ourselves. In this book, I share clear and simple tools to interject into your day for rest and meditation. We already have so much information about how to work out. This is more of a guidebook for how to work in. We learn how to build our muscles, yet we are rarely provided with tools for cultivating the ability to sit peacefully with ourselves.

I believe we all truly want to feel good and be kind to ourselves—and sometimes, it's just a matter of shifting our perception and accessing simple tools that help us transform from within. Before we can transform perspective, however, we need to access the part of us that can observe and step back to see the bigger picture.

There is an exorbitant collection of literature available now about consciousness: what it is, where it is stored, and how we access it. Neuroscientists especially are curious about how it is that we humans have the unique ability to observe ourselves in such a way that we do not get wrapped up in our storytelling and the whirlwind of accompanying emotions. Experienced meditators are known for their capacity to step into a space within themselves from which they can simply observe, without judging or analyzing. This vantage point brings great peace to the practitioner.

This is the greatest gift that yoga offers humanity: the ability to step into this space. What I deeply appreciate is that there isn't only one way—there are many ways, and depending on what you need, the tools of yoga will meet you where you are.

Along with offering you some of yoga's most important tools, I offer the perspective of whole-self-care. The term *whole self* acknowledges that we are willing to examine all the layers of ourselves. We begin the journey of understanding the whole self by considering its many aspects. Following this understanding, it is your choice if you want to take care of your whole self. I cannot force you, only inspire you. It is your sovereign right to choose.

Ultimately, you have the power—and now, the tools—to shift out of the constant state of stress to which so many of us are accustomed. You can make a dramatic change that impacts not only your life, but your entire world.

Yoga and My Journey to Human Being

I have been living as a human being for 45 years. I am a born seeker who devoted my first 20 years to spiritual inquiry by looking outside myself to institutions. In the later part of my life, I spent my time and energy on the realization that the greatest inquiry one can undertake is made by looking inside.

I grew up in a split household, spending the week at my father's home and weekends with my mother and extended family. As a child, I gravitated to family members who spoke differently and were not caught up in the daily churn of their pain and the constant game of "he said/she said." These numbered just a few people: my father, my grandfather, and my aunt. Their elevated advice to me impacted my ability to see beyond the superficial layers of life and hold a standard around self-inquiry that I didn't learn anywhere else. I was active in the church, starting in high school and through my early twenties. However, the more I studied the Bible in its original text, the less I saw it embodied in the people around me.

My spirit of inquiry continued but was compromised by other life circumstances, including my marriage. I was married for 16 years and raised two beautiful boys. I participated in my marriage about half the time; during the other half, I observed it with disbelief. I began to observe things I had no prior experience with, so I didn't know how to digest or investigate them. In that relationship, I often felt immobilized and incapable of responding to my spouse's behavior; I would only later recognize this state as one of shock.

Ultimately, I tuned into all of my layers (physically, energetically, mentally, emotionally, and sensually) and realized that I'd ignored some major aspects of our relationship to keep the marriage going. Overall, I could see that my layers were not in alignment.

One summer, when I had some time to be alone, I realized I had compartmentalized aspects of myself—and it was time for a reunion with my whole self. So I began to care for my whole self, which led me to another realization: I had been living in a state of dissociation in my home life and a state of integration in my spiritual life. It was time to get these aspects of my life on the same page. I did not have to do this by demonizing my husband or casting myself as a victim in the marriage; I realized that I could move toward change in ways that celebrated my whole self. I eventually freed myself and my husband by filing for a divorce. I am grateful to live in a time during which this is possible and people can make a conscious choice in favor of their well-being and life energy.

I continue to be humbled by the lessons that life brings my way, and how they inspire me to attune to the layers of my whole self. Currently, my 16-year-old younger son is my foremost teacher. As I tune into his brain and nervous system, I see how I can extend more compassion than judgment, and how I can choose to engage with him from a place of genuine curiosity and inquiry rather than assuming that I have the answers in advance (a tactic that, by the way, does not work with teenagers!). I recognize that the world he navigates is different from mine, and I understand that many teenagers are dealing with elevated levels of anxiety that are instigated by our hectic and troubled world. So I have learned to tread with kindness and demonstrate love in a radically different way.

Luckily, I have always had a helpful companion along the path of self-inquiry and love. Yoga has been with me since my early twenties and has provided me with access to a great companion within myself. I refer to her as the *Queeeeen*. She is calm and joyful; she is gorgeous and simple; she is unfailingly observant yet able to pick up the sword of love as needed; and she is constantly discovering how to best take care of her realm. In yoga, this companion is simply called *atman*.

The language of yoga is Sanskrit, mathematical in design and poetic in expression. Each word often contains a minimum of seven definitions. Thus, *atman* has multiple meanings, although the one referred to most in yoga is "essence, individual soul, or a timeless aspect of oneself."

Yoga offers a method to develop a relationship with atman that is not intended to conflict with a person's religion, cultural upbringing, gender, age, or abilities. (In fact, the frequency of love I have experienced from Christ, Mary, and St. Teresa of Avila remains very important to me, and has only become more acute as I have practiced yoga.) The main reason to practice yoga, as it has been for millennia, is to relieve suffering.

Nowadays, our phones, cars, computers, and the overall rhythm of our lives are calling us to be some sort of super machine...not a human being. The drive to becoming a super machine has invited me to ask the following questions: Does this mean we are supposed to multi-task to no end? Are we being called to go, go, go for 12 hours straight and never pause to rest or nap? Are we to ignore our basic needs of human connection, emotional safety, and kindness to achieve a level of success that society has deemed the ultimate goal?

Instead of *doing* so much, what if we focused on being amazing human *beings*?

The Vedic teachings of ancient India share that our journey in life will guide us through being animal, human, or divine. Before becoming divine, we must become fully human. What does this mean? It means we need to return to our essence, love, and bring our whole self back into alignment with the frequency of love, not the frequency of our multi-tasked lives, ever-changing technology, and over-active egos.

Through my work with yoga teachers and practitioners, I have found that if we can activate a few tools and keep inviting pauses to the nervous system, we can avoid a lot of suffering. I have seen countless individuals move away from being slaves to this accelerated modern lifestyle to feeling a sense of peace within themselves, strength in their abilities, and wisdom in their decisions. How does this happen? By taking time to purposefully pause, breathe, move, and meditate.

These days, we literally run ourselves into the ground. This doesn't hurt only us—it sets a precedent for generations to come. Our children are susceptible and impressionable; they learn through our actions. The legacy we are leaving with respect to our well-being is in question. How do we define this for the next generation? It cannot only be the physical side of our existence that gets defined, measured, and studied.

We have an undercurrent of mental health issues in the United States that no one wants to face, and that few have offered viable solutions for. Why else are we choosing substances and opioids as our primary self-care tools? For three years in a row, the Centers for Disease Control have noted that life expectancy is decreasing. In 2018, the reason for this was opioid-related deaths. I am determined to be part of the solution that increases our life expectancy so our children can look forward to progress in health and wealth in our unstable and inequitable society.

This is why I have written this book: to share with you the tools that invite the care of the whole self. The care of the whole self is essential, and throughout this book, we will discuss in detail what I mean by the whole self—as well as how we can tend to it with care and love. I recognize it is not easy to address all our layers every day, but there is a way! The methodology offered by yoga is brilliant and simple. Throughout this book, you will find a number of yogic tools that can be accessed any time of day for the care of the whole self. The tools I highlight in this book all come from time-tested practices that are backed by science. I have also shared resources at the end of the book for you to further your own study and inquiry.

Andrew Harvey's perspective on sacred activism inspires me every day. Sacred activism is born from passion that is rooted in heartache. Andrew says, "If you're really listening, if you're awake to the poignant beauty of the world, your heart breaks regularly. In fact, your heart is made to break; its purpose is to burst open again and again so that it can hold evermore wonders." So in the midst of my heartache for the human story right now, I am deeply motivated to share the tools of yoga so that you can be empowered to take care of yourselves in the midst of an era that is not inspiring us to do so. All the yoga-based tools are offered in 1–3-minute practices that are simple and accessible. If you have 1–3 minutes to invest in your well-being every day, let's continue! May you be inspired, encouraged, and profoundly motivated to make wise, informed decisions for the love of yourself and for your family, friends, and communities.

The Wisdom of Poetry

As I travel through this life, I find that I choose to engage more and more in poetic discourse with myself. The heart of the poet is my core. I work hard to express in linear ways my thoughts, musings, and learnings, but poetry is where I feel most liberated in my expression.

I swim in the world of yoga. I read the Vedas, Upanishads, Tantras, Puranas, Bhagavad Gita, and Yoga Sutras. All of these sacred Sanskrit texts are constructed in poetic verse with a mathematical foundation of rhythm.

Poetry is one of the greatest tools of communication humans have created, and a great differentiator between us and the animal kingdom. Poetry as an art form can only be found among the human species. It is a way to speak to what is unspeakable, to express what cannot be expressed but only felt.

The beauty it offers reveals the ultimate freedom that we can harness from creative expression.

Poetry is purposefully designed to explain what is unexplainable due to the rules of poetry. In short, there are no rules! You can create rhythms, meters, and rhymes, and then you can simply let them go. You can utilize no punctuation at all. You can do away with pronouns and verbs. And somehow, you can still ensure that it makes sense. You can scatter words across the page and convey feeling. You can speak in metaphors and convey what you are attempting to say with more clarity than if you'd spelled it out in plain and unembellished language.

This book is composed of words. Sometimes you will read them as clear explanations, and other times you will be offered a pause in the form of poetry. We can't always go to the ocean of wisdom. Some days, we need to pause by the fresh spring of poetry and take a sip. Enjoy pausing!

I closed my eyes
and could see clearly

Like a stone that recognizes its own river
laying itself down
welcoming the waters to flow
around and smooth
its corners

I closed my eyes and dropped into
the unnamable

Yet I recognized it like
the hands of my grandfather
life living in his veins
skin leathered from life
yet the timeless pulse of his soul is intact

A felt experience
that only poets have the courage to speak to
and scientists scurry away from
the force that poets allow space for in between their words
and scientists spend eons defining

Soul speakers the poets are
If you feel it needs to be defined
then open your eyes and read about it
in the spaces between the words

14

Chapter One: Self-Care in Hectic Times

"Self-care is giving the world the best of you instead of what's left of you."
Katie Reed

There is a part of me that would love to create a marketing campaign across the United States, using billboards and TV ads to communicate one message: Your Nervous System Is Under Attack—Practice Care for the Whole Self!

There is no doubt about it: Our nervous systems are truly under siege in the United States. I believe this shift occurred sometime after 9/11, when CNN and other networks changed the way they share news. We went from looking at one person speaking and sharing information to a continuously streaming line of text on the screen (often stating tragic or disturbing news) alongside columns to the left filled with other randomly related information. Our eyes became accustomed to scanning the screen continuously as our brains began multi-tasking at a new level.

This shift continued to move into other areas of our lives, and the scrolling was translated to what we do when we are on social media, with so many distinct parcels of information vying for our attention. Most recently, the new shackles we wear around our wrists under the guise of a health and wellness monitor have begun to keep us in a state of constant hyper-alertness to all the things we "do." This includes how we sleep, how many steps we take, and whether or not our activities are measuring up to our ideas of who we should be. In our day-to-day lives, when technology has become a constant source of scrutiny, everything is being analyzed and judged.

While some of the effects of these tools might be seen as positive upon first glance (e.g., Facebook gives us the opportunity to connect with old friends, and a Fitbit helps us to gauge our level of activity), the end result is almost always a kind of fatigue, sometimes even depression and overwhelm. If it is connection and health that we're looking for, it seems unlikely that we will find them in our current technology.

We are losing one of the greatest tools humans have: our intrinsic ability to look within, check in with ourselves, contemplate, and inquire internally. We are overly focused on external results and productivity, to the detriment of our rich internal landscape. Think about it: When was the last time you closed your eyes or looked into a mirror and simply said, "How are you?"

If you can, I encourage you to take a pause from reading this and do so right now. Perhaps you'd like to place a hand over your heart as you gaze at yourself and take three deep restorative breaths. As you slow down to simply scan your body for thoughts, emotions, and sensations, how does this feel? Are you accustomed to taking this time to compassionately be with yourself, just as a loving parent would with a child? Or does it feel awkward and unfamiliar to you? If it does, indeed, feel strange to you, it could simply be that it's time to gradually shift your attention from your regular habits and preoccupations to coming back to yourself. I encourage setting a recurring timer of sorts that allows you opportunities for spacious self-inquiry. There is no explicit "point" to such an activity, such as weight loss or catching up on current events. However, the value of simple and consistent check-ins cannot be underestimated. They are worth their weight in gold, and when added up, you will find that they are priceless.

Why Is Self-Care Essential?

We live in a culture that glorifies and perpetuates stress. In 2018, *Everyday Health* surveyed 6,700 Americans nationwide, ages 18 to 64, to find out what causes stress and to determine how we cope. The results were interesting: 51% of women and 34% of men reported that they feel bad about their appearance; 52% said that financial issues regularly stress them out; and 35% shared that jobs and careers are common stressors. How do we cope with the stress? 47% percent stated that their response to stress is to take it out on themselves!

The science of stress illuminates that stress that continues for an extended period of time (three months or more), known as chronic stress, can have major implications on the well-being of a person. Stress places pressure on our nervous and endocrine systems. Can there be good stress? Yes. But when we wear down our nervous and endocrine systems, we also wear down our immunity, resiliency, and capacity to handle and manage stress: physically, emotionally, mentally, and energetically.

Stress shifts the inner landscape by releasing a surge of hormones into the body. What gets these hormones to stop producing is the invitation to states of rest, relaxation, restoration, and safety. I will be sharing some effective tools with you throughout this book to invite such states with ease and compassion, as well as self-care.

Self-care is becoming more and more essential for our well-being. We often arrive at this realization after an illness, a diagnosis, or trauma. We often engage in self-care habits out of the fear of getting sick, instead of from a place of love for ourselves. Often, it is only when we become dis-eased or sick that we begin to make choices that are more in alignment with maintaining our well-being. While illness can be a powerful initiator into the importance of self-care and healthy living, a downward spiral in our health is not requisite in order for us to act lovingly and mindfully toward ourselves.

When it comes to our well-being, my teacher Sri Mohan always states that the most important limb in Patanjali's eight limbs of yoga is *dharana*, the ability to pay attention. Sadly, I find that our current world is doing an excellent job of teaching us how to *not* pay attention. We need to fight hard to even watch the news; as I've mentioned, on a typical TV screen, news is simultaneously streamed at the bottom, on the side, and then across the headlines associated with what the news reporter is speaking about.

We expect life to be a journey of multitasking. Although many employers will stress the importance of multitasking in any given role, the exacting toll of spreading ourselves thin across a range of tasks and stimuli is becoming more and more apparent. We know now more than ever that our brains can multitask, but we cannot actually pay attention to multiple things at one time. At any given time, our brain is managing internal temperature, electrolytes, amino acids, neurons, and more. However, despite our brain's magnificent automatic abilities, we can only consciously pay attention to one thing at a time.

According to one researcher, high multitaskers are inefficient at pretty much everything that is necessary for multitasking to begin with! When we attempt to do several things at once, our brain's capacity to do any of them is reduced substantially. Multitasking not only slows us down, but research also suggests that it can lower our IQ.

How can we begin to minimize the negative consequences of multitasking? By slowing down our frenetic pace and giving ourselves fully to one or two tasks. Zen practitioners and other students of Eastern religions have often written about the power of being fully absorbed in a single task, whether that is washing dishes or putting one foot before another. This kind of attentiveness has the power to bring our systems into equilibrium, recalibrate our peace, and lead us to moments of powerful insight and connection with ourselves and all living beings.

We have been revolting
for so long

It is not working

I study
extracting from the center of "revolt"
a four-letter word
LOVE

It's time to evolve
Aha!
It's been here all along
Why didn't I see it

What has been coloring my lens all this time
Now I see clearly
Love

      "Build upon me," Love said
      "I will feed you from my bosom"
      "I will build you shelter with my heart and mind"
      "Holding you like a lover, my Beloveds"

      "Please don't turn away," she called out louder this time
      "I will share my wisdom only to awaken your own wisdom"
      "I will guide and never force"
      "I will love you through the pain"

      "Let me hold your hand," she passionately lifted her voice
      "Don't drown"
      "Don't lose hope"
      "I am here for you, My Beloved Ones"

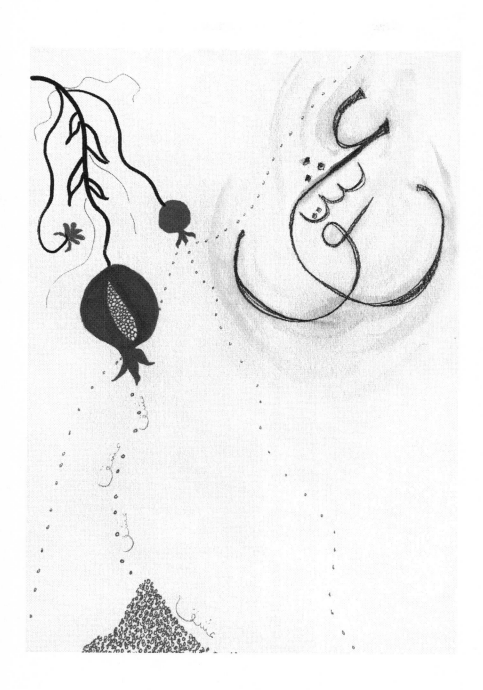

The Role of Trauma-Informed Therapies

I have designed the book and its practices to be trauma-informed. You see, at the heart of many of the epidemics that plague our society, including suicide and addictions, you are sure to find trauma. Trauma is the result of deep hurt that could have begun a few generations past, in the womb, due to the lack of kind and loving parents and caregivers, or because of experiences of violence and abuse as a victim and/or observer. Often, because we haven't been given tools for how to interact with ourselves in a nurturing and caring way, we literally don't know how to cope with the traumas we experience and see in our households, schools, and society.

We live in a time during which the word *trauma* is a part of our daily vernacular. We have trauma-informed schools, trauma-informed yoga, trauma-sensitive psychotherapists, trauma-sensitive health practitioners, and so on. I am grateful to live be part of a field of emerging yoga teachers who call themselves trauma-informed. However, I also know that this reveals something very striking about our era—that is, our nervous systems have been violated, attacked, and abused to such a degree that our social frameworks have adjusted to our violated nervous systems. We must do whatever we can to heal this, but we must also acknowledge the root causes of our suffering and choose to move in a direction that restores us to our epicenter of peace, calmness, and joy.

Later in the book, I will define the nervous system more clearly. For now, just understand that it's the main regulator of all the systems in your body. It absorbs information, assesses it, and tries to find ways to maintain homeostasis. Homeostasis is a term used in the medical world to describe a self-regulating process for maintaining stability in the body. For example, when we feel very hot, we sweat in order to try to cool our body. This is a homeostatic process. The body's constant attempt to achieve homeostasis is an enormous task, because like peace, it is not a permanent state. It fluctuates, expands, contracts, and meets the moment.

I absolutely believe that unless you choose to befriend your whole self, you will most likely succumb to some form of imbalance or dis-ease. As resilient as the nervous system is, it is also fragile. The care of the whole self is imperative to us our progress in creating a society that is calm, balanced, and peaceful. I believe this is possible. It starts with you, and more specifically, with how you care for *your* whole self.

In my annual course on Trauma-Informed Yoga, co-developed with fellow yoga teacher Heather Hagaman, we share four keystone principles that I utilize as guidelines for the practices I offer. I've listed them for you below so that you can take them into your own self-care practices.

- Choice is power. Make conscious choices that support your whole self.
- Commit to a focus on the present moment through body orientation, breath, and awareness of your sensations.
- Use rhythmic, repetitive, and holding methodologies to support toning the vagus nerve and nervous system.
- Activate joyful, awe-filled curiosity!

The sound wouldn't let up
in my sleep
in my wakefulness
in my spaces of contemplation

It remained
a strange hum cry
no harmony
no rhythm
erratic
discordant
piercing

So instead of listening, I decided to create
to string sounds into harmony
to create spaces between the pulses for rhythm
and infuse it with my own unique vibration

And then do you know what happened!?
Coherence
Resonance
Harmony
Peace

24

25

You Are Worthy of Care

This book has been created to support humanity in remembering what it means to be fully animal, human, and divine. Yes, we are indeed all of them. Our animal self is invested in survival, while our human self wants to experience joy and pleasure and our divine self wants to live in such a way that we are of benevolent service to others.

Science's insight into neurogenesis (the birth of new neurons) and neuroplasticity (the malleability of neural circuits) has revealed to us that it is possible to undo old habits and create new ones. While stress in the form of emotional, physical, and environmental stimuli can greatly impact and hinder our ability to birth new neurons or develop healthy neural circuits, a number of activities—from yoga to mindfulness meditation to repeating positive affirmations—can help us rewire our neurobiology and our seemingly permanent belief system so that we can move in the direction of embracing our full potential.

If you have doubts about your own potential and intrinsic value, consider the following.

We are made of star stuff. Our bodies literally contain atoms that have existed from the moment of the Big Bang. We are nature made conscious. Trees breathe in what we cannot and give us the nutrients we require. Bees pollinate flowers to give us food. We are all connected in an intricate and delicate web of life-affirming symbiosis. We must learn to honor rather than abuse these relationships, whether with nature or people. We must share with those who need it, inspire each other, and take care of what is precious.

Do you consider yourself worthy of care, like the trees, bees, and other human beings?

If we look around at our world right now, we are heading in a trajectory that is reflecting the danger of treating ourselves, each other, and our planet with carelessness. Can you hear the call of our planet? She is crying out to us: "Is this what you want? Look what you did when you weren't aware of how special our home is. Isn't your body your home, too?"

Care begins with the simple yet profound choice to pay attention to the consequences of your actions. These might include the consequences of scrolling on Facebook longer than you'd intended...having that extra glass of wine with dinner, which ends up disrupting your sleep and making you wake up feeling groggy or depressed...choosing to turn on the news and be bogged down in the endless stream of talking heads spreading doom and gloom. There are so many seemingly minor choice points that occur throughout our day that we take for granted. When we opt in favor of mind-numbing and body-desensitizing activities, we are making the choice not to care for ourselves, even if this is not a conscious decision of ours.

In this moment, I want you to notice whether your mind is restless or unable to maintain a focus for three minutes. Without the ability to focus your mind, true self-care and peace will be unattainable. Likewise, you can absolutely maintain a constant state of peace, tranquility, joy, and unbounded love, as long as you develop the skill of remaining focused and devoted with your intention. It may sound like a new-age platitude; however, it is old age, what I call an original teaching. This ancient belief is at the heart of the philosophy of yoga.

What ultimately keeps us from peace? Ourselves.

This is a harrowing truth, but we do have the power to change it.

If you are a seeker with a desire to awaken yourself and therefore your communities and societies, then continue reading.

It's completely up to you.

However, before you choose, let me share...

It won't be easy.

It will require you to be fully present.

It will often necessitate that you go against the grain and fight the tide of distractions that looms everywhere around you.

You will need to have faith.

You will need to unmoor your attention from the external factors that have served to hijack it.

You will need to take action.

You will be asked to take care of yourself and inspire others, simply by being you and returning to what is most essential.

You will be called to love and to share the essence of who you are.

When you learn to practice the tenets of whole-self-care, you will begin to naturally extend compassion and recognize our interconnectedness.

You will be motivated to smile more, to see the beauty in everything and everyone, and to serve those who need help as well as those who are suffering.

You will identify a burning desire to contribute to building a society that reflects what we have always known is possible in our hearts.

You will be a catalyst for change.

The choice is yours.

Convoluted dimensions wrap around me

I follow each thread only to be led to the other

Eventually I find my way back home
as though each one was a clue

How generous
not just one clue
but multiple
in case I get lost

There is always a way back home

Chapter Two: What Whole-Self-Care Isn't—and What It Is

"Neti neti: In Hinduism, and in particular Jnana Yoga and Advaita Vedanta, neti neti (नेति नेति) is a Sanskrit expression which means 'not this, not that,' or 'neither this, nor that'…The purpose of the exercise is to negate rationalizations and other distractions from the non-conceptual meditative awareness of reality."
Wikipedia

A tool used in yogic analysis is the tool of negation, also known as *neti neti* (not this, not that). We basically spend time understanding an idea or concept by understanding what it is *not*. This is how we ultimately dive into understanding what is meant by whole-self-care: that is, by first understanding what it is *not*.

We can begin by examining some of the unhealthy negative behaviors that plague our society and that eventually become untended habits. We have learned to hide from ourselves. We hide behind labels and responsibilities. We hide behind our busy-ness and are afraid to acknowledge our emotions. We are afraid to look into mirrors and make eye contact with others when in conversation. We expose parts of ourselves and keep other aspects hidden, and then we wonder why we don't feel seen, heard, and touched. We act one way at work, another way at home, and then another way with friends. We are literally being pulled apart, and we are making a choice to be this way, because it is either what we have seen modeled or it is the only way we know how to remain safe.

The idea of self-care has fallen prey to this way of being in the world. It has been reduced to a marketing gimmick and a way to sell massages, spa weekend getaways, and even happy hours at your favorite local bar. We have turned self-care into tools for checking out versus checking in. It has become an excuse to over-consume and numb ourselves, instead of a framework to acknowledge and nourish our entire being.

Nourishing one's entire being requires feeding all parts of the self. I often encounter people working out hard in gyms, running marathons, and engaged in physically challenging activities, yet they actively avoid meditation and anything that would require them to sit with themselves quietly, in stillness, and explore the field of the mind.

At the other end, I also know meditators who sit for several hours a day in silent meditation and are frozen in their ability to feel and express their emotions.

I also often observe people taking care of themselves by eating healthy or paying attention to their waistline, only to go out and poison themselves with drugs and alcohol in order to let off some steam. I have also encountered supposedly legitimate programs that take advantage of this binge-and-purge mentality. Take Detox to Retox, which combines celebrity workouts, healthy cuisine, and partying—feeding off the myth that when it comes to our well-being, we can have our cake and eat it, too; that is, we can pour time and money into our physical health and appearance, only to load toxins back into ourselves in the name of well-deserved fun.

This is the slippery slope self-care is on, and this is what self-care is not.

Why is this a big deal? I believe it is a big deal because at some point it all catches up with us. Around us are all the signs that what we have been doing hasn't been working. In the United States alone, chronic disease at an all-time high.

This is why, for the purposes of this book, we are using the term *whole-self-care*. The title of the book is the *Care of the Whole Self* to emphasize the necessity of providing an attitude of care towards all aspects of our journey.

This is not a one-dimensional exploration. What makes this book radical is that you are being asked to acknowledge every aspect of yourself, and it can be done through active engagement three times a day for five minutes at a time. Doable? Absolutely. If you are struggling to take three minutes in the morning, afternoon, and evening, then this book may not be for you, but you might need to make some important shifts in your life.

What Is Whole-Self-Care?

Our well-being and vitality are found in being fully present in our wholeness, all the while practicing the guiding principles of compassion, clarity, and generosity. We release our scarcity mentality, which keeps us in a constant cycle of grasping and over-consuming, and we recognize that there is enough for everyone. We nourish all of ourselves and naturally take care of each other.

Those who are leaders, have decision-making power, and are in the eyes and ears of many especially need to pay attention to their whole-self-care.

I have run a yoga studio for over 15 years, and from the beginning, I knew that if I didn't show up for myself first and foremost, I was going to burn out and become the quintessential stressed-out yoga studio owner. I didn't want this to be my legacy. I deeply believe in this practice, philosophy, and process called yoga, and I live it. If I didn't, I would feel like a fraud. Authenticity is my guide.

In order to be authentic, we must ensure that all aspects of our being are aligned and congruent. In yoga, there is a well-known framework known as *panchamaya*, the five illusions. This framework is from the Upanishads, a Vedic body of work several thousands of years old. The framework acknowledges that we have different layers that are all interrelated. Our enlightenment arrives when we live in alignment with all the layers and recognize they are all a part of us even though they need not ultimately define us. Our happiness, joy, and peace will be found in our ability to manage our fear and make decisions that are in alignment with the best version of ourselves: our whole self.

The source text of the panchamaya framework is the Taittiriya Upanishad (written sometime in the sixth century BCE). Here is an excerpt:

> *Human beings consist of a material body built from the food they eat. Those who care for this body are nourished by the universe itself.*
>
> *Inside this is another body made of life energy. It fills the physical body and takes its shape. Those who treat this vital force as divine experience excellent health and longevity because this energy is the source of physical life.*
>
> *Within the vital force is yet another body, this one made of thought energy. It fills the two denser bodies and has*

the same shape. Those who understand and control the mental body are no longer afflicted by fear.

Deeper still lies another body comprised of intellect. It permeates the three denser bodies and assumes the same form. Those who establish their awareness here free themselves from unhealthy thoughts and actions, and develop the self-control necessary to achieve their goals.

Hidden inside it is yet a subtler body, composed of pure joy. It pervades the other bodies and shares the same shape. It is experienced as joy, delight, and bliss.

Our peace is a byproduct of not hiding anymore and being able to fully embrace ourselves. In yoga, self-care is the method of seeing all the dimensions and layers of oneself and taking care of them because they all reflect something very precious.

The genius of another capstone framework of the yoga method is called *ashtanga*, which is the eight-limb path developed by the sage Patanjali (mentioned in the Introduction of this book). Each limb acknowledges a layer of our humanness and invokes a thoughtful relationship with each of our layers.

- *Yamas*: Guiding principles toward the external realm
- *Niyamas*: Guiding principles toward the internal realm
- *Asanas*: Postures (what many people tend to think of as yoga)
- *Pranayama*: Breath practices that liberate prana
- *Pratyahara*: Conscious repurposing of our senses
- *Dharana:* Focus and concentration
- *Dhyana:* Meditative absorption
- *Samadhi:* Peacefully integrated experience of the whole self

Overall, the eight limbs offer specific guidelines on living a meaningful, purposeful life that offers us the highest state of awareness. Patanjali believed that with dedication, mastering the eight limbs can enable us to gain healthy control over our lives so that we are able to express the fullest extent of our physical, mental, emotional, and spiritual potential.

Today, the eight limbs remain a powerful framework for reminding us of the need for activities and routines that generate balance and peace in our lives.

Yoga Technology

The body has kept scientists, doctors, and researchers of all fields very busy and will continue to do so—because we still have so much to learn. Our body is what I call a living eco-matrix: an interdependent web of tissues, electricity, hormones, and neurotransmitters all wrapped up in an electromagnetic field that we do not fully understand. From its codification in the Vedas, Upanishads, Yoga Sutras, and countless other texts, yoga has equipped us with the technology we need to overcome the greatest journey we can embark on as human beings: overcoming suffering and remaining fully intact in our peaceful, joyful center.

The tools to access this center are breathwork, movement, and mindfulness practices such as meditation.

What makes this complicated is that the perfect state for all the systems to run optimally is unique to each of us and is impacted by environment, relationships, food, exercise, and our individual life experiences and personal histories.

I am amazed at the amount of funding that has been invested into understanding how meditation works, and why having a daily breath practice matters. While a scientific understanding can help to further legitimize these practices, I believe we should be focusing instead on giving all humans access to these tools and incorporating them into our children's education.

I will be the first to admit: Yoga isn't for everyone. People with certain physical limitations, such as arthritis or herniated disks, will have to be diligent about finding instructors who are capable of meeting their unique needs. Moreover, although yoga has become increasingly popular in the West, not all practitioners are choosing to benefit from a deeper understanding of this sophisticated spiritual framework.

True yoga, when it is practiced with respectful attention to the ancient tenets underlying it, is about spiritual exploration and discovery of the subtle life energies that make up one's being, as well as the universe. It's about discernment and learning to differentiate between what changes and what is constant.

What is constant? That is the individual journey of discovery. In Sanskrit, it has a name, *atman*. So what is atman? Like most Sanskrit words, it is very challenging to translate. I offer you a simple definition: the aspect of yourself that is peaceful and unchanging.

In every yoga teacher training I lead, there is always the need to discuss whether or not yoga is a religion. It is not. It's a means to support anyone in lessening their suffering, regardless of their religious orientation. I believe everything we learn in life is a theory. So I invite you to consider yoga as a theory. Test it and see if it is true for you, and if you are able to access a constant, peaceful space within yourself.

It's important to remember that yoga has its origins in spiritual practice, and people who relegate it to merely a form of physical exercise designed to increase our heart rate and tone our abs are missing the point. It is true that some people will simply not be interested in delving deeper into the philosophy behind yoga (which I argue is an essential aspect of practicing yoga). However, I believe that yoga has universal wisdom to offer.

In this book, I offer a framework, inspired by yoga and also reinterpreted to meet you in today's world. Let's explore these dimensions together.

The image of the seed sprouting into form has been used for thousands of years to depict the human story and struggle of moving from the darkness of our mysterious origins and into the light of our full manifestation (enLIGHTenment). I use it here to represent the layers of the whole self. The whole self comprises the following:

- Seed and roots: Physical self
- Stem: Energetic self
- Buds: Mental self
- Leaves: Emotional self
- Blossoms: Sensual self

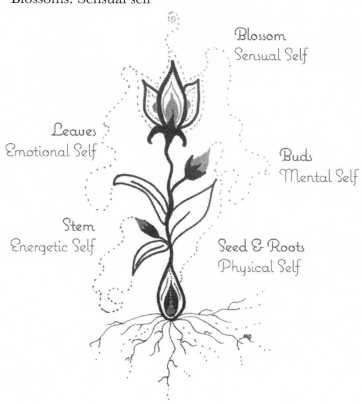

Blossom
Sensual Self

Leaves
Emotional Self

Buds
Mental Self

Stem
Energetic Self

Seed & Roots
Physical Self

I do not include *spirituality* here, as I don't believe it is an aspect of us.

In yoga, the experience of spiritual awakening is described as *samadhi*, a peaceful absorption of the integrated self. There are many types of samadhi described in the Yoga Sutras of Patanjali. The essence of all of these forms is that samadhi is a state in which our sense of being is fully integrated, connected, and absorbed—not to mention, free from suffering.

It's clear that the experience of samadhi, to which so many spiritual seekers aspire, can only be realized when we know ourselves as fully integrated, with all dimensions of ourselves seamlessly interconnected.

You cannot appreciate only the blossom without the seed. You cannot understand the potential that exists in a seed without seeing the blossom. When you have trained your attention to recognize the vital importance of the entire organism of your being, you will have an experience of full integration, which is synonymous with what most people think of as spirituality.

Part 1:

I have been sitting for thousands of years
waiting for this body, this time, this place

I arrived miraculously
against so many odds
I arrived intact
a soul in a body

Spending 45 years looking around
I still can't make sense of this

Yet I know this is precious
so I hold it
with tenderness
with kindness
with a kind of reverence
that reminds me over and over again
of the Divine Grace that resides
within me

Part 2:

If my Soul had eyes
how would it look upon this world

The Soul can only see one way

Its gaze is
            singular
            eternal

unitive
both a wave and a particle

Its pulls in information
for only one purpose
to remember how to Love

Chapter Three: Dimensions of the Whole Self

"Most psychologists treat the mind as disembodied, a phenomenon with little or no connection to the physical body. Conversely, physicians treat the body with no regard to the mind or the emotions. But the body and mind are not separate, and we cannot treat one without the other."
Dr. Candace Pert

The Upanishads encourage a return to the whole self, a timeless aspect of yourself that is separate from the ego, which aims for perfection. Wholeness is always available to us in the present moment, as a complete understanding of our true identity. When we embrace our wholeness, we relinquish the delusions and illusions that keep us stuck in narrow definitions of who we are and who we should be. Thus, it is wise to accept *all* the dimensions of who you are without getting stuck in any of them.

The dimensions of the self I am sharing here are inspired by panchamaya (or the five illusions), and I have expanded on them in greater detail in this chapter.

According to panchamaya, there are five *koshas*, or five sheaths of our being: the physical body, the energy body, the mental-emotional body, the wisdom body, and the bliss body. They are referred to as illusions not because they are "unreal," per se, but because we often have a tendency to mistakenly identify any one of them as our true self. In actuality, our true self encompasses these different "bodies," but it is so much more than the sum of its parts.

These dimensions of the self are interrelated and connected. Understanding that they are interrelated invites the knowledge that if you work with one, you will ultimately impact all layers of the self. Being aware of this may help you make wiser decisions. When we ignore our innate wisdom, we tend to repeat cycles of habits that continue to make us feel disconnected. When we are clear about the dimensions of the self and work to integrate them in our awareness, we make decisions that respect them all— and we also arrive at a deeper understanding of the workings of the universe and the oneness that is behind all phenomena.

I debated on whether to call this book *Care for the Whole Self During Stressful Times*. This is because I deeply feel and know that if we do not take care of ourselves, especially during stressful times, we can inevitably land in the hands of substances and develop violent ways to cope in the interior landscape of the mind. So as we dive into the dimensions of the whole self, it's important to acknowledge that there may be hurts embedded in each of them. This is completely normal, and we must offer ourselves compassion. If the process feels overwhelming, call a friend or seek a professional, such as a psychotherapist. Then begin with small steps to learn tools to care for your whole self with acceptance and kindness.

Look inside
You imagine I am full of rolling fields of moss
sweet blooming bluebells
yet my life has invited
more horrific plantings in the garden of my mind

Each day I go to my garden
weed
plant
and sit to enjoy the landscape
sometimes looking over my compost pile
to remember what was thrown away to transform into this
gorgeous
lush
beautiful
bountiful
blissful
garden
I am

The Physical Dimension of the Whole Self

A man had enrolled in a yoga teacher training at my studio. He was an ultra-runner, which meant he ran 50+ miles at a time. He loved yoga and what it offered him. He shared with me a phenomenon that often happens with ultra-distance athletes; that is, usually somewhere between mile 50 and 70, he would experience vision loss. He shared how this would happen to him regularly without any explanation. He would recover after a few hours or a few days.

I asked him, "Do you think this is a sign that your body is giving you to not run these distances?"

It was a frozen and heavy moment. I almost wished I hadn't said anything, as I understood right then and there that his drive to run these distances was so much greater that anything his physical body had to say. I thought about this for days and weeks and saw how his physical body was giving him palpable signs that weren't enough for him to overcome his drive to be an ultra-runner. I backed down and realized that the self-care experience for him would be limited until he could embrace his physical layer with compassion and love.

He eventually moved on, and yoga was not able to maintain a presence in his life.

The day after I wrote this section of the book, he reached out after five years of absence to say that he wanted to finish his teacher training. I cannot help but feel that my sharing his story invited him back to look inward and pick up where he left off—to experience his physical self as a peaceful liberator rather than a source of consternation and imprisonment.

He told me that he is still running but is now retired, so he has the time to step into the seat of the yoga teacher. When he shared his desire to complete his teacher training, I smiled to myself and contemplated how life happens on terms that are often not our own.

When I talk to him, I will once again ask the question, "Do you think this is a sign that your body is giving you to not run these distances?" I look forward to hearing his response.

Food and the Elements

What do I mean when I speak about the physical dimension? I am talking about organs, skin, tissues, muscles, bones—in short, all the tangible matter that you are made of.

As we progress through the layers of the self, you will see how the physical body contains all our layers. However, it is often the easiest to deal with. This is why I believe allopathic medicine stays in the lane of the physical. (We don't have energy doctors at a hospital, do we?)

In Ayurveda, the ancient Indian holistic system of medicine and health, the body is made up of five basic elements: earth, water, fire, air, and ether.

For a moment, I will shift to this lens of considering our layers in elemental language, since our body is made up primarily of water, which is a conductor, insulator, and solvent. It's one of the most powerful elements, and without it, we would not have life! So, if we look at this understanding of the body, we will see that the brain and heart are composed of 73% water, and the lungs are about 83% water. The skin contains 64% water, muscles and kidneys are 79%, and even the bones are watery at a whopping 31%. When we engage in activities that take our finely calibrated elemental makeup out of balance, our physical bodies suffer as a consequence. When the physical body is in pain or out of balance, it speaks quite loudly to us. It becomes red, hot with inflammation, and it extends sensation-based frequencies that the mind interprets and medicine defines in categories of illness and disease.

Interestingly, although we are speaking about it first, the physical body is considered the last layer of manifestation, according to Hindu philosophy. Manifestation of what? Suffering! The imbalance begins at a more subtle layer, and it is only until we can see it that we begin to pay attention. In Sanskrit, this layer is called the *annamaya* (literally, the food layer). Think about it—the foods that we eat give us the building blocks for the matter of our bodies. This is why the saying, "You are what you eat!" rings so true.

When considering the physical dimension, looking at your diet is equally as important as looking at how much you exercise, sleep, and practice yoga. My teacher, Sri Mohan, states that you can meditate and practice yoga, but this does not necessarily mean that you will make real progress—that is, until you examine your diet. Ultimately, what we eat affects the building blocks of our body and mind and can impact how we think.

As far as food goes, I want to offer some guidance and perhaps controversial insight. I have found that people who sustain vegan diets for more than ten years without proper supplementation of protein and minerals often deal with neurological imbalances. In a 2017 article in *Psychology Today*, Dr. Georgia Ede writes:

> *Vegan diets contain virtually no vitamin B12, and severe, prolonged B12 (as well as amino acids) deficiency is fatal. Most vegans and vegetarians are aware of this danger and either take supplements or consume fortified yeast (unfortified yeast doesn't naturally contain any vitamin B12). Unfortunately, deficiency is still far more common than it should be, with some studies finding that as many as 86% of adults (regardless of chosen diet) are deficient. Researchers report wide ranges of values, but overall, vegetarians tend to*

have lower B12 levels than omnivores, and vegans on average tend to have the lowest B12 levels.

Ayurveda is a balanced holistic framework that looks closely at habits around diet, lifestyle, and physical and mental activity. The medicinal aspects of Ayurveda lie in utilizing herbs, diet, and lifestyle habits. Yoga is an important part of Ayurveda. However, I do not see Ayurveda being an active part of yoga and how yoga is practiced. I believe yoga practitioners would reap some of the healing benefits of yoga by utilizing the awareness of the Ayurvedic lens.

The Ayurvedic diet is a mostly vegetarian diet containing cheese, yogurt, and ghee (all dairy-based). Often, at different stages of life, organ meats and meat may be necessary to consume. I believe it's important not to take a fundamentalist or rigid approach, and I have made it a practice to honor what is best for the individual. Often, narrow attitudes toward eating can create a sense of despondency, guilt, and shame. We are often taught by diet culture to judge ourselves on the basis of what we eat, but a strict regimen is seldom sustainable and can negatively impact our overall well-being.

I encourage my students, and you, to take a more measured approach to food. You can choose to learn about nutrition, but it is best to go with easily applied, time-honored principles than fad diets that are overly restrictive or reductive.

One of the most important journeys you will take in life will be with your food. Eating is the first instinct we have as a baby. Once born, a baby is placed on a mother's belly and crawls up to the breast to be nourished. We seek it in *everything*: our relationships, our work, our home, and our food. For food to be nourishing, it must support your optimal well-being and offer you what you need to think with clarity, move with ease, and digest peacefully.

Later in the book, I will share the concept of interoception and how yoga is beneficial in developing this system so that we can attune to our body's feedback system of hunger, thirst, and fullness, all of which are integral to our nourishment.

I have a deep personal connection to the many facets of nourishing ourselves. In college, I started to remove all fats from my diet. I experienced a lot of anxiety and did not have a menstrual cycle for two years.

I saw several doctors, and not one of them at that time inquired about my diet. In retrospect, I wish they had. I started to do my own research. I also began to incorporate breath practice to manage my anxiety, started taking an herb that was used in Germany to treat a condition similar to mine, got my cycle back, and then started to study more holistic modalities. I was well aware that I had paid a price for my eating imbalance. I realized I couldn't get hungry, and I felt better when I didn't eat. I ended up seeing an integrative doctor, and after doing thorough blood and stool tests, I discovered I hardly had any hydrochloric acid in my system to break down the food.

As I started to rebuild my system, my appetite came back and I naturally started to eat in a way more attuned to something known as intermittent fasting, which is all the rage these days but is actually synonymous to the Indian holistic system of Ayurveda. Ayurveda has always supported rest for the mind, body, and digestion. The balance of eating and fasting is very, very important. If you are interested, I encourage you to seek an Ayurvedic practitioner to support your journey.

It is crucial to understand that our eating habits always have an emotional component that goes back to the time when we were in utero and receiving nourishment from our mothers' bodies. Eating is a highly emotional experience, and it's okay that it is. If we continue to ignore this truth, then we can easily overlook our eating imbalances. If you suspect that you might be suffering from eating imbalances and disorders such as anorexia or bulimia, please seek help and begin paying close attention to how you nourish yourself.

Unfortunately, many eating disorders arise from the fact that we can be quite extreme with ourselves. Keto diets and excessive protein-based diets have their negative long-term effects, including weight gain, constipation and other digestive disorders, bad breath, dehydration, kidney damage, heart disease, and even increased cancer risk. Moreover, the dilemmas that we face over GMO-based foods, excessive sugar, and foods grown through pesticide use are real.

In this book, I want to offer you a starting platform. Here are my guidelines.

Eight Essential Nourishment Guidelines for the Care of the Whole Self

- Eat whole fresh food: food closest to the earth, not from a box or freezer.
- Be more plant-based and watch your intake of proteins and minerals.
- Have a daily fast of 12 hours between dinner and breakfast.
- In hotter weather, eat more raw food. In colder weather, eat more cooked food.
- Chew your food, and limit juicing and shakes (which wear down your digestive system and our enzymes); the less we chew our food, the less we digest/absorb.
- Eat foods that are in season.
- Use spices and herbs to flavor your recipes.
- Spicy food agitates the digestive lining. Less is best.

I will be offering more tools in the self-care section about ways to interact with your food to cultivate care of the whole self.

Of course, food is only one component of the physical self, and as I mentioned in the introduction to this section, fitness and exercise are another component that could warrant an entire book! The bottom line when it comes to our bodies is this: We must learn to pay attention to the sophisticated cues that our body is offering us—whether this is in the form of hunger or satiety, pain or comfort, etc. The body is truly a temple, and when we learn to use yogic and other tools that enable us to develop a dialogue with it, we truly pay homage at the basic altar of our being.

Absorbing the world
I take it in
trusting the nourishment that is fed

Closing my eyes
I trust the world
I take it in

Then, one day the body says no
You can't take that in
or that
or this
and definitely not that
but you can take this
oh and that
You can absorb this way
but not that

The body knows something
so I humbly listen
because I love

Lover

54

The Energetic Dimension of the Whole Self

In quantum physics, the energy that surrounds and moves through all living things, including our planet, is called the toroidal energetic field, which surrounds the magnetic field. This toroidal field has a strong central axis and is maintained through a coherent field from the bottom to the top. It is said that the field surrounds the Earth, and that 90% of the field emanates from inside the Earth.

The same is true for the field that surrounds us as human beings. Its coherence begins inside us, especially with the energy surrounding the heart, which is said to have the strongest and largest energetic field in and around the human body.

In the language of yoga, the energy that pervades all things is called *prana*. It is the one thing that unites all of life. In essence, we are breathing the same energy the dinosaurs breathed—it has simply gone through some transformations, but the essential life force has been circulating for eons.

The energetic layer of the body is known as *pranamaya* in Sanskrit (or, a layer of life force that is always moving). Prana in the body is carried through matter and in pathways known as *nadis* (rivers). While there is no counterpart to prana in Western medicine, it is prana that travels through your tissues, organs, and muscles and keep you alive. Prana travels through your nervous system, makes your heart beat, and is the source of life within you. Thoughts, senses, and systems of awareness also utilize prana.

The most powerful and influential tool we have for managing our energy is our breath. In Sanskrit, breathwork is called *pranayama* (literally, a path to liberate our prana). In Ayurveda, a framework known as the *gunas* is used to explain the qualities of prana. The gunas, according to Ayurveda, have always been present in all material phenomena.

The three primary guna qualities are: *sattva* (which represents radiant embodied wisdom), *rajas* (which represents passion and excessive activity), and *tamas* (which represents dullness and inertia). Every single being contains each of the gunas, and it is the specific interplay of *gunas* that determines the basic nature of everything we encounter. According to the ancients, it is possible to balance our gunas (for example, if we have too much rajas or tamas) by practicing pranayama.

This helps us understand that prana can continuously expand. Whereas your physical dimensions can deteriorate, your energetic dimension can expand. Neurons are the vehicle through which the mind processes actions and thoughts. We can maintain vitality in our energetic dimensions by engaging in learning, feelings of awe and wonder, and meditation. The entire premise of yoga is that the body will decay, but the mind can continue to expand. Remember this and you can avoid a lot of future suffering.

Another important dimension of the energetic layer is our emotions. Emotions are essentially frequencies that transform the biochemical landscape of the body. Anger will begin to flood the body with certain neurotransmitters, and love will flood others. The mind will label these emotions, but they are simply biochemical vibrations.

Joshua Freedman writes about Dr. Candace Pert's pivotal work in science and emotions, stating, "Emotions, Pert explains, are not simply a chemical in the brain. They are electrochemical signals that affect the chemistry and electricity of every cell in the body. The body's electrical state is modulated by emotions, changing the world within the body. In turn, Pert finds emotional states affect the world outside the body."

A tool in tantric yoga, known as *rasa sadhana* (or the study of the essence of emotion) can be used to understand the emotions. I was first introduced to it by Peter Marchand. The basic idea is that rasa sadhana is a process of "emotional fasting," wherein we commit ourselves to ceasing engagement with one of the less desirable *rasas*, or emotions, and engaging more fully with one of the more pleasant *rasas*. The point isn't to be rigid about forcing ourselves to feel specific emotions; the simple act of remembering our commitment can help us to dissolve and cut through the clutter of painful emotions and to experience greater peace.

Below is a diagram I created. In short, the entire range of human experience is organized into nine rasas. Peace is in the center (*shanta/shanti*), because it is the essence associated with the natural self. Peace was later added to the framework of the rasas. I suspect the original Tantric teachers didn't think it needed to be separated, but eventually, it was evident that it needed to be named.

I view shanta as the great rasa, the one we use our tools to come back to time and time again, which is why it is placed in the center. We want to experience the full range of emotions, but we don't want to linger in any of them too long…except for peace. That is the entry point to our essence.

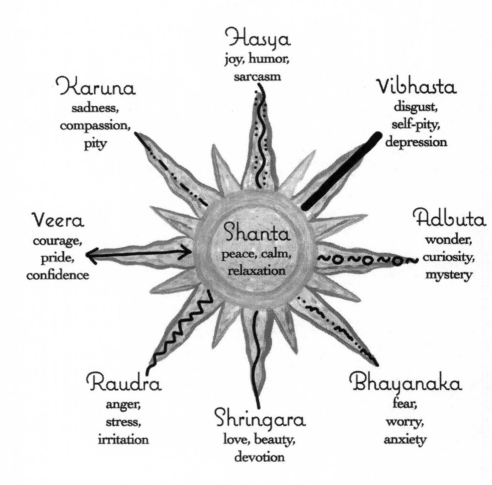

Hasya
joy, humor,
sarcasm

Karuna
sadness,
compassion,
pity

Vibhasta
disgust,
self-pity,
depression

Veera
courage,
pride,
confidence

Shanta
peace, calm,
relaxation

Adbuta
wonder,
curiosity,
mystery

Raudra
anger,
stress,
irritation

Shringara
love, beauty,
devotion

Bhayanaka
fear,
worry,
anxiety

Three Energetic Guidelines for Care of the Whole Self

It's important for you to understand three guidelines as you approach energy at this point in your journey for the care of the whole self:

- Like attracts like.
- Opposites heal.
- It all depends.

Here is a story to illuminate these guidelines: Imagine a person—let's name her Julie—has a very fast, active life with very little down time. Between work and family, there is a lot of activity that cannot be changed right now. We would look at Julie's life rhythm as being *rajasic*. She eats behind her desk at work and tends to skip breakfast. However, she tries to sit with her family at least three to four times a week for meals.

Now, Julie attempts to incorporate self-care into her schedule four times a week; she has decided to go to a gym and start running, spinning, and lifting weights. The gym environment is active, with lots of noise. We would see the gym as a rajasic space.

Julie has been experiencing a high level of chronic stress. She is unable to fully sleep at night and notices a bit of agitation in herself. A friend mentions yoga, so she decides to start with private yoga sessions.

There are a lot of factors that can't all be looked at through this case study. However, I will summarize. Because her life is rajasic and now her self-care plan is also rajasic, the guideline of "like attracts like" will manifest in all layers of Julie's life. There is nothing wrong with her life rhythm or her self-care. But because there are symptoms of imbalance manifesting, including chronic stress evidenced by symptoms of sleeplessness and agitation, we will apply the guideline of "opposites heal."

You might recognize Julie in yourself or people you know. When I began working with Julie, we started to shift her routine, adding simple self-care at the beginning of her day that embodied qualities of the sattvic aspect of the gunas. I didn't ask her to change anything—we just added 15 minutes of smooth, simple movements with breathwork and a three-minute contemplative practice to her evening, to support her calming down for sleep.

Yoga is a practice that meets each person where they are. We are offered frameworks to approach well-being and peace. In Ayurveda, this state is called *svastha*, or the well-being of the whole self.

Yoga is a practice, process, and state wherein an individual journeys toward their stable center and is able to remain centered through the fluctuations of life. All frameworks of yoga are similar, yet they offer a diversity of perspectives that support the expansion of the whole self.

Pulsing shots of hydrogen
atoms filled with electric charge
gather around the vibrating orbs
all trying to find their way to the great mighty universe
where the fields have no edge
and there is comfort with no day or night

There is a center point
where we all meet
This place feels refreshing
refreshing like the sip of cold watermelon juice on a hot summer day

Pausing, I looked in again
experiencing energy like a familiar companion
that I had forgotten
but never lost

The Mental Dimension of the Whole Self

The mental dimension houses all aspects of the mind. In Sanskrit, this layer is called *manomaya*.

Considered one of the subtlest dimensions and the hardest to manage, the mind is often considered only after dealing with the physical and energetic dimensions.

We still have much to learn about the mind, including how exactly it works, as well as where consciousness and awareness rest in the mind. In yoga psychology, thoughts are categorized into five groups: valid knowledge, misconception, imagination, sleep, and memory. Then there are four other aspects of the mind: *manas*, the aspect that takes in information from the senses; *citta*, the aspect that takes the information and holds it as important (embedded thoughts); *asmita*, the aspect that protects (ego); and *buddhi*, the aspect that discerns (wise self).

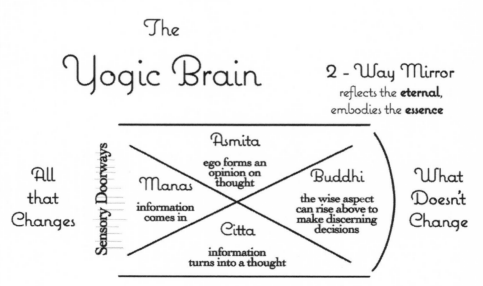

The

Yogic Brain

2 - Way Mirror
reflects the **eternal**,
embodies the **essence**

All that Changes

Sensory Doorways

Asmita
ego forms an opinion on thought

Manas
information comes in

Buddhi
the wise aspect can rise above to make discerning decisions

What Doesn't Change

Citta
information turns into a thought

I have a client whose worry-based anxiety is literally creating memory loss and symptoms of dementia. He came to me after three months of dealing with this. He'd already seen an integrative doctor, neurologist, psychiatrist, acupuncturist, and psychotherapist. The anxiety was not getting better.

The anxiety began after an aggressive antibiotic treatment that may have gone a few weeks too long. This unsettled state in his digestive system and body created a perfect terrain for unsettled thoughts to flourish like bacteria, and they did.

In his journey of recovery, which took several months, I didn't want to get into the stories behind the worried thoughts. I knew that without a disciplined daily practice of breathwork, he would not be able to stabilize his nervous system and cultivate a terrain of ease for himself to manage the worry-based anxiety.

We explored left-nostril breathing three times a day (which I explain in detail in the self-care tool section) for 90 seconds at a time, each time he took his medication.

After a month of this time of practice, his anxiety calmed. I cannot say it was all due to the breath. However, I do know he made a significant shift with the addition of the breathwork!

The level of the mind can be beneficial or detrimental to us—it all depends on how we train ourselves. Yoga is, of course, designed, to bring out the highest functions of manomaya. But because the mind has been conditioned to constantly make judgments and analyze our experiences, this commentary can hinder our development of the higher functions. Often, we become caught up in our negative or harsh thoughts, believing these to be absolutely objective and true.

During a yoga or meditation practice, we will likely experience many of these thoughts: *I'm so distracted—I can't do anything right...I'm never going to be able to hold this asana, so I should just give up....I wish I had a yoga body like hers—I'm so fat in comparison...I don't think this teacher knows what she's doing...I'm a better yogi than him, and my body is so much stronger...This is boring and I just want it to end!*

Throughout the day, and even throughout our contemplative practices, we will find ourselves caught in judgments, assumptions, and difficult emotions, but it's important to remember that part of integrating the mind into our whole-self-care is about using this as an opportunity to practice compassionate awareness. In simply noticing our judgments with compassion, we can learn to move with ease into the subtle layers of manomaya.

It is helpful to incorporate pranayama, asana, and *drishti* (gazing upon a concentrated point to maintain presence and attention) to train our minds, rather than getting pulled this way and that way by our mental fabrications and stories about what we are feeling and experiencing. The more we do this, the more we will notice the internal chatter decreasing in its loudness. As it falls away, we can remain steady and focused, and compassionate witnesses to everything that is unfolding within and around us.

The ability to remove ourselves from unhelpful thought patterns, which can contribute to both physical and emotional ill health, is one of the most valuable aspects of yoga. The point is not to remove ourselves forcefully, but to do so with kindness and loving compassion; from this place, we acknowledge what is and choose to focus on what brings us closer to our peaceful self. Given how powerful the mind is, and the fact that so many of us swirl in the often-chaotic mental layer, it is important to allow our mind to become a friendly companion rather than an enemy.

Aside from yoga and meditation, there are many other ways to train our minds. Offering the manomaya rest in the form of sleep is essential to our well-being. (Ever noticed that lack of sleep can result in mental fog and crankiness the next morning?) The mind is tasked with a number of small and major tasks throughout the day, from making simple decisions to performing complex calculations. If we are tired or sleep-deprived, we place an undue burden on our minds.

Overall, just like the other layers, we must take the time to pay conscious attention to how our minds are operating on a daily basis. Without our attention, the mind reverts to autopilot and habits that may not serve us. It takes mental willpower to shift our habits and to move into a state of witnessing rather than identifying with our thoughts. When we dedicate ourselves to nourishing the mental layer of our being, we begin to make better choices about our self-care and overall lives.

Think of this process as an act of intentional decluttering. We are removing our attention from the mental debris that so often flits through our consciousness without our awareness, and we are choosing where to focus. Another example of training the mind is mantra repetition. Repeating a mantra or phrase can allow the incessant, ruminating mind to simply rest and rejuvenate itself. It's akin to a mental detox, and the more we practice it, the more benefits we will reap. Likewise, filling our lives with positive and stimulating (but not overstimulating!) people, environments, situations, and activities can offer our minds a great deal of nurturance that will prevent us from falling back into unhelpful habits.

The mental layer of the self is extremely powerful, and we must remember that the way we use it matters. The words that we speak to ourselves and others matter. The manner in which we absorb and integrate truth also matters. Instead of deluding ourselves with spiritual bypassing, such as insisting, "I'm not my emotions or my body," we can use the mind to exercised discernment and dig into the truth of what we are experiencing. To engage with this layer of the self, we are exercising the willingness to open up to the entirety of our human experience, and to use our whole intelligence to do this.

She held my hand
that little girl
who whispered dreams and ideas
which seemed unimaginable to my conditioned mind

The wise one reached out to hold her hand
and listened to the visions of places
that felt like home
even though
I knew them not

The Emotional Dimension of the Whole Self

In the Rig Veda, one of the oldest Indo-Iranian texts about life and creation, it is taught that there are many creation stories. It suggests that we pick one that meets our culture, family, and society, while understanding that all creation stories emerge from love. In fact, love is the foundation of all creation, so it is not necessary to get stuck on the story—instead, we must remember the message behind the story.

If we apply this to ourselves for a moment, let us consider that our entire existence is based on love. How radical is that? Sometimes, we are born into situations that are the opposite, and I believe this is to ultimately help us become even stronger lovers in this world.

In addressing our emotional dimension, we need to understand the role that all emotions play. However, there are three emotions that essential to master for the care of the whole self: love, peace, and joy. The soil that cultivates them all, and the place to begin nurturing them in our own lives, is gratitude.

I believe we need to speak more to love in our daily lives. We need to be courageous in our conversations and challenge each other in dialogue about this essential human emotion. Yet, love is so challenging and uncomfortable for many of us to openly discuss. That is why, in my opinion, poetry is the greatest conduit to explain the unexplainable, including deeply mystical experiences and emotions like love. One of the great poems to speak to the unspeakable nature of love is by Khalil Gibran, who ironically was an alcoholic and died early from this disease. I cannot overlook that perhaps it was his suffering that allowed him to speak so eloquently about love and other universal human emotions. He spoke of what he longed for, and his addiction was his only way to remain in this world long enough to share his wisdom.

Here is an excerpt from his epic poem, "On Love":

Think not you can direct the course of love, for love, if it
*   finds you worthy, directs your course.*
Love has no other desire but to fulfill itself.
But if you love and must needs have desires, let these be your
*   desires:*
To melt and be like a running brook that sings its melody to
*   the night.*
To know the pain of too much tenderness.
To be wounded by your own understanding of love;
And to bleed willingly and joyfully.
To wake at dawn with a winged heart and give thanks for
*   another day of loving;*
To rest at the noon hour and meditate love's ecstasy;
To return home at eventide with gratitude;
And then to sleep with a prayer for the beloved in your heart
*   and a song of praise upon your lips.*

The Three Hurts

There is a teaching in yoga that states that all our suffering comes from three hurts: not being heard, seen, or touched with value and respect.

It is also said that these three hurts are sourced from one suffering we all share in common: not being loved.

Think of a child who is born unwanted, and whose parents are unable to offer love in tangible ways. The child is left to cry themselves to sleep; they gradually learn coping tools and even master the ability to disassociate and move inwards for safety. Even if shelter, water, and food are provided, it cannot replace this essential human experience: to be loved.

What happens to a child who grows up like this? We have so much evidence of what happens to children who experience neglect and abandonment. It's deeply tragic, yet it happens every day. We haven't even added the top three categories of abuse: verbal, sexual, and/or emotional. In my opinion, abandonment is a form of all three major categories of abuse.

The emotional dimension of the self needs attention. We must begin by understanding our individual ability to love and be loved. The greatest experience as a human is to love.

If we always remember that love is the highest aspiration of the human/divine soul, we learn to look at more difficult emotions—anger, rage, grief, confusion—through the lens of love.

As I mentioned in the section on the mental self, in order to train our minds, we must practice attention to our thoughts, which create our stories. Emotions are not the same as thoughts, although we often confuse them for each other. Emotions are feelings and inner body sensations to which we then apply meaning. The most important thing we can do with our emotions is to give them the utmost compassion.

The tantric text known as the Vijnana Bhairava addresses the highest states of consciousness, and how we can wed our human awareness to divine awareness. This powerful text states that we can do this by including absolutely everything in our experience, even emotional pain. This sense of inclusion is precisely what allows for transmutation and healing.

Many yogic and tantric texts speak about the power of living from the heart (which not coincidentally, is tied to the element of space, suggesting a greater sense of spaciousness). True enlightenment is the recognition that even our so-called "negative" emotions, when held with compassion and from the vantage point of the compassionate witness, can be transmuted in the light of *atman*. We are all made of the same energy as the divine source, and everything in our existence is specially designed to help us remember this. By distilling emotions to their energetic essence, we naturally create movement. In fact, emotion is meant to be moved through our bodies. The act of running, stretching, jumping, can change our feelings without our having to do anything (another reason yoga is so powerful). Even assuming a new posture can take us from a state of feeling dejected to feeling more confident.

At the same time, while we might be searching for a way out of uncomfortable emotions, there is nowhere we need to "get to." Many of us long to be in a state of love and bliss all the time, but the truth is, we cannot force ourselves into such a state; forcing anything is counteractive to the nature of love. By offering love and spaciousness to all our emotions, rather than acting them out, we can simply allow them to dissolve into the vastness of consciousness. Like our thoughts, we need not be pulled this way and that way by our emotions, and nor do we need to act on them. We can simply allow them a space for internal expression and transformation with our loving attention. We can view our difficult emotions as gateways to love and bliss, even though they may not seem to be so at first glance.

In dealing with difficult emotions, it can be helpful to follow a simple process of witnessing and allowing them to be:

- **Notice what you are feeling.** Sometimes it can help to simply pause in an intense moment and give voice to what you are feeling. What are the body sensations associated with the feeling? Are you angry? Sad? In grief? Say the emotion out loud to yourself, or internally. Rather than jumping into stories, be with what is happening. Get to the deeper layer of the emotion.
- **Breathe.** Often, we will want to either act on what we are feeling or stuff it down in order to diffuse the intensity. Instead, pause and take several deep breaths, simply paying attention to your inhalation and exhalation. If you are

feeling a charge of energy, do a few cycles of smoothly inhaling through the nose and exhaling through pursed lips to calm the nerves. Eventually, you will want to transition into easeful nostril breathing. Note whether this changes the intensity of your initial emotion, or whether the emotion itself dissipates.

- **Ground yourself.** We often tend to forget our bodies when we are in the throes of very strong emotions. It can help to simply place a hand over our heart as we breathe, or to lightly tap our bodies from head to toe to maintain a sense of connection to ourselves in the present moment. The simplest way to ground is to check your feet and note where they are! This will automatically bring you back to an awareness of your body.

- **Focus on your heart center.** This isn't just about focusing on your physical heart space (which is still undoubtedly quite powerful, as it contains the largest energy field in the body), but on the subtle space of your inner awareness where you feel the presence of love and peace. Even if it feels extremely miniscule, invite yourselves to believe for a moment that it is there.

- **Take time to explore the nuances of what you are feeling.** Perhaps the feeling has grown or taken on a texture, temperature, or specific "flavor." Explore it. Let yourself feel the sensations more acutely, knowing that it is safe to do so.

- **Notice any stories that come up and allow them to simply sail through your awareness like clouds in the sky.** Understandably, we may find ourselves getting caught in stories that ensnare us in defensiveness or intensify our emotions. Before you allow this interruption to get out of hand, you can practice letting go, perhaps even visualizing the thoughtforms melting into the thin air upon each exhalation.

- **Allow your heart to hold whatever you are feeling.**
  Bring your awareness back to the emotion at hand. Let
  your heart space be a vast and compassionate container for
  your emotion. Imagine holding it with tender love. It's okay
  if you don't feel an obvious shift. You are not attempting to
  make yourself feel better or more comfortable. You are
  simply training yourself to respond to your emotions with
  compassion and acceptance rather than turning away from
  them or acting out. The more you do this practice, the
  more you will experience ease and feel empowered to face
  the challenges of life.

Holding intense feelings can be difficult but training
ourselves through somatic practices such as the one above can help
us to unlock the energy of these emotions and use them as fuel for
our journey toward wholeness.

The Sensual Dimension of the Whole Self

As I waited for the light to turn red, the conversation with the
homeless man on the corner started out simply enough. I asked,
"How often are you on this corner?"

"I have been in shelters for a while now, but so happy the
weather is good today. It was really hard last week." He then
began to share how he got to be homeless, saying that he just
couldn't take being on 30 mg of Paxil a day. He couldn't take what
it was doing to him. He raised his arms into the air and said
dramatically, "I couldn't have sex!"

He then explained that if you don't take your medication
for three months, insurance cuts you off, and the checks stop
coming—which led me to assume he was on some sort of disability.

The light turned green and I drove off, saying to him, "May you be blessed."

As I later reflected upon this chance encounter, it was clear to me that the simple desires of our humanness can take us over completely. The inability to feel and connect intimately with another was this man's poison. The medication that was helping him, however, was also numbing his sensuality. So I had to ask myself: Was he lost in desire, or by refusing the medication, was he simply standing up for his right to maintain some aspect of his humanness with dignity? Moreover, can we find ways to support and uplift each other so that we always have access to the basic dimensions of our humanness?

The sexual imbalances in our society are becoming more and more evident. We live in a culture in which sex is plastered all over our billboards and screens, but we have no idea how to address sex and sensuality in healthy, open ways, through constructive and non-shaming dialogue. There even is a Sex Addicts Anonymous (SAA), unaffiliated with Alcoholics Anonymous (AA) but inspired by the original 12-step group. Whenever you see such a large support system in place, it often points to a very real and significant problem in our society. The #MeToo movement made it absolutely evident that we have years and years of hidden sexual traumas that individuals have carried for decades. These experiences lead to both sexual imbalance and sensual deprivation.

In the search for freedom, the pendulum often swings to extremes. We become extremely liberal before becoming extremely conservative, or vice versa. We must pay close attention to our perspective and intention. Many of us feel we can claim our power by being sexually liberated or by indulging in hedonism, yet we still experience sensual starvation. We have sex to achieve a climax but can feel completely numb right after. The bottom line is, we are sensually starved as a society.

Sensuality is associated with the second chakra, related to creativity, pleasure, and enjoyment. This is not merely about sexual gratification. We are naturally sensual beings, blessed with finely attuned senses. Although we may have been taught that this is bad or even "evil," our sensuality is an important aspect of our creative potential. Repressing our natural instincts can compromise our access to a sense of safety, joy, and full expression.

Connecting to ourselves and others involves and requires being in *touch* with our senses. One of the eight limbs of yoga, as I have mentioned, is *pratyahara*. Pratyahara highlights the role and power the senses have and the associated necessity to have mastery over them so that they can help us connect deeply to ourselves and others.

In my opinion, an essential aspect of tuning into our sensual self is to get back to nature. Unfortunately, we don't have a sufficient amount of clinical peer-reviewed studies that demonstrate the tangible importance of reconnecting to nature, and how it puts us in touch with our own essential humanness. However, through my private work, as well as through my knowledge of nature-based movements, I have seen the return of emotional interconnectedness and sensuality through intimate contact with nature. By "intimate," I mean being in touch with nature…literally.

I live in a city called Reston, a planned community that was founded on the vision of the American real-estate entrepreneur Robert E. Simon. Nature was designed into the city plans. In 2018, Reston became officially designated as a biophilic city. The term *biophilic* refers to a concept in the design industry that is used by architects and planners to help us feel connected to our natural environment.

The designation is given by The Biophilic Cities Network, which was founded by Tim Beatley, a professor of urban and environmental planning at the University of Virginia. Beatley wrote, "We carry with us ancient brains, and to be happy and healthy and have meaningful lives, we need that connection with nature. And we can't just get it on a holiday for a week or two during summer. It has to be integrated into our daily lives—everyday nature where we live and work. Nature we experience every hour."

The more we connect with concrete buildings, screens, and silver-plated technology, the less we will connect with human touch. The more we straighten out rivers into concrete walled dams, the less we will remember the sinuous natural flow of a river and the fishes that swim along or against its current. The higher our heels and the more covered our feet, the less we understand sensation at the soles of our feet. Pausing at the start of our day and placing our feet on the earth are ways we can remember our sensual self. So is exploring the moment of contact with the moist, cool earth or the hot sand of the desert. The soles of our feet are entry points for energy and life. Hands are the same. For those who live in high rises or far from the ground—hold the leaves of your plants and greet them every day. Connect to life in its purest form.

Yoga teaches that our relationship with our breath will attune our senses to the present moment. I believe this connection to the present is an intimate sensual experience that allows us to touch the essence of life.

I will offer specific suggestions for connecting with the sensual dimension in the self-care section. For now, I would like to share what I do as a daily practice. I am surrounded by orchids in my home. They have been blooming for over seven years. I greet them each morning, starting my day with awe and wonder. I hold one blossom in my hand, gaze at it, breathe several rounds of a breath (inhale, gentle pause, exhale, gentle pause), and say hello. I notice how the orchid has exposed its most vulnerable parts with so much beauty and grace.

I aim to live life with the same vulnerable strength. To live life with strength is not enough, though. It is only one aspect. In the teachings of yoga, ease and softness are celebrated just as much as the unwavering steadiness of strength and courage.

It is not enough for me to just gaze at the orchid—it is also crucial to touch. Our sensory system of touch is a huge part of our well-being. We know that babies that are not touched will die. Maia Szalavitz writes, "Babies who are not held, nuzzled, and hugged enough can stop growing, and if the situation lasts long enough, even die."

In Ayurveda, daily habits of self-massage to feet, hands, face, and/or body are actively encouraged. The important stimulation this offers the largest organ of our body hasn't fully been revealed by contemporary studies as of yet. Likewise, engagement practices with nature involve touching the earth, plants, and trees...literally getting "in touch" with nature. It's not only about taking daily walks on the trail or stopping to hug a tree. Lay down and place your body against the ground, hold the leaves and plants in your hands, and use your sense of touch to sensually connect to yourself and to what you are made of.

The emotional and sensual dimensions of ourselves need our utmost attention. So often, we fall prey to addictive behaviors such as compulsive shopping, excessive Internet or porn use, excessive drinking or drugging, and other things that are a clear cry for help indicating that we have lost contact with our essential self.

Get back to nature, touch nature, and let it speak to you. It sounds so simple, and it is. The self-care toolkit at the end of the book invites simple ways to engage with nature daily, and also offers essential self-massage instruction.

The Integrated Peaceful Dimension of the Whole Self

When one experiences the integration of all the previous dimensions of the whole self that I have discussed, this leads to a natural experience of "spirituality." When all aspects, dimensions, and/or parts of the self dissolve and become absorbed into a singular, unitive, peaceful existence, we find ourselves being born into the spiritual dimension.

The spiritual dimension is not a separate dimension—it is the culmination of all of the previous dimensions I have mentioned. It is not something that needs to be nurtured separately. I believe the compartmentalization of spirituality in the Western world has been a cause of much suffering. Placing the responsibility of spiritual discourse in the hands of religion is one of the great downfalls of humanity. It has created such a sense of separation within society and within ourselves. Ironically, we can collectively live spiritually fulfilled lives if we live integrated within ourselves, our households, our workplaces, and our communities.

When we live integrated lives, connected to our whole self, we take a major step toward building a healthy and spiritually mature society and country, free from dis-ease.

I have found that many students who reject any form of God or religion experience spirituality through the integrated peaceful state of the whole self. When the self becomes sacred, this is reflected in our lives. Our inner technology has been set up this way, and it is our superpower; that is, by attuning to ourselves, we attune to each other.

How is a piano tuned? By having a tuning instrument nearby to resonate with it. This is the awesome and overwhelming power each person has.

How are you going to get in touch with this power? How are you going to take care of it? How are you going to use it?

My desire burned so deeply
Tears filled my eyes as I slammed my hands against the earth
and asked,
"Why can't you tell me the truth?"
I tried so many ways
I chased…I followed
I led
I failed
I studied
I surrendered, and finally I found it
I stepped away
and saw it all
the whole thing
perfectly clear

Chapter Four:
Calibrating Your
Nervous System

"For breath is life, and if you breathe well, you will live long on Earth."
Sanskrit proverb

Today, we know unequivocally that the breath is the most powerful tool for managing one's nervous system. Breath management tools are now part of so many systems, from centering students in schools to training Navy Seals.

Breathing works because of the physiological effect it has on the nervous system. Breathing slowly and deeply activates the hypothalamus, which is connected to the pituitary gland. The brain is stimulated to send out neurohormones that block stress hormones such as cortisol and adrenaline from being released. This triggers a relaxing response in the body. Additionally, breathing deeply and slowly triggers the parasympathetic nervous system to secrete hormones that decrease blood pressure and heart rate, which also induces a relaxation response in the body. This is done mainly by the way of the vagus nerve, the main controller of the parasympathetic system.

Dr. Stephen Porges' polyvagal theory has impacted our perspective on the nervous system more than anything else in the last 20 years. Prior to this, Dr. Herbert Benson's work in the 60s and 70s on the relaxation response was monumental. Below is a basic overview of these two concepts that are essential for everyone to know.

Polyvagal Theory and the Relaxation Response

Lisa had been practicing yoga for decades and just experienced a car accident. She had no physical injuries. However, since the accident, she had been feeling very internally disconnected. Although nothing was broken, her sense of safety had been hijacked. She was agitated whenever she drove, as well as in silence and times of rest.

I asked her, "How do you start your day?"

"Well, because I manage an international team at work, I wake up and check my phone to see what is going up, catch up with news, and then, after a bit, get out of bed."

I responded, "What if you took a few minutes before you look at your phone to open your eyes, get in your body, and simply say thank you to the day or anything you would like to extend gratitude towards?"

She agreed, and it shifted her morning. I offered her a morning routine and this simple tool of how to start the day. It's all about getting "online" by getting "offline."

The way we start our day teaches our nervous system how we want to navigate. If you start the day with a go-go-go attitude, analyzing everything outside of yourself, your nervous system will most likely remain in a sympathetic state. The sympathetic nervous system triggers the fight-or-flight response. Ideally, this happens only when you are responding to actual danger, but given the number of stressors in people's day-to-day lives, it can be triggered by something as annoying yet harmless as a person cutting you off in traffic.

Your nervous system manages everything, especially your hormones. Based on what the nervous system picks up, it will stimulate the release of certain hormones. For example, remaining in the highly analytical sympathetic state, scanning for threats, and leaving no space for rest can stimulate the overproduction of cortisol. Cortisol is a neurotransmitter that's known as the stress hormone. It's an important part of your internal alarm system as it alerts the amygdala, the part of the brain that detects stress in your environment. The tiny but almighty amygdala is our emotional processor. Particularly responsive to stressful stimuli, the amygdala can trigger our freeze-fight-or-flight response.

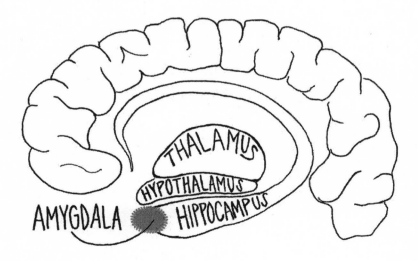

Cortisol also does a lot of wonderful things. For example, it:

- Manages how your body uses carbohydrates, fats, and proteins
- Keeps inflammation down
- Regulates your blood pressure
- Increases your blood sugar (glucose)
- Controls your sleep/wake cycle
- Boosts energy so you can handle stress and restores balance afterward

However, while the positive benefits of cortisol are important to keep in mind, it's also true that our fight-or-flight response is often unnecessarily activated. As I mentioned earlier in the book, many of us live in a high-alert, constantly stimulated state. We are constantly reacting to perceived dangers in our environment that may not deserve our full attention.

Keeping yourself in the sympathetic system all day is like keeping your alarm clock buzzing all the time! If you start the day contemplatively, inwardly focused on something positive, you will stimulate the parasympathetic system. This is also known as the rest and digest system, as it helps us conserve energy and promotes the relaxation response in the body.

It takes devotion to whole-self-care to balance out the world we live in and pursue the desire we have for peace. It is through the power of choice that we overcome our animalistic, ego-centered survival instinct and enter the realm of conscious decision-making for not just ourselves, but for others, as well. Going back to the example of Lisa, she made the choice to get her whole self integrated before supporting her family.

Our nervous system is a beautiful, elegant system of communication nestled into every corner of the body. Science continues to provide us with insights into the nervous system every day. The nervous system takes information gathered from the senses and other systems of the body and makes decisions to help keep the entire being intact and alive!

An important aspect of understanding the entire nervous system is understanding the role of the vagus nerve. The vagus nerve has a number of powerful functions, including helping our brains form new neurons; turning off the fight-or-flight response through the activation of the relaxation response; blocking system-wide inflammation, which can contribute to aging and poor help; helping us overcome depression and anxiety; aiding in better sleep; turning down allergic responses; and contributing to our overall well-being. The vagus nerve is connected to our parasympathetic nervous system. When we engage in activities like deep breathing, we essentially work to alleviate the detrimental effects of the sympathetic nervous system.

Dr. Stephen Porges' polyvagal theory (PVT) expanded our perspective of the vagus nerve and the nervous system like nothing else in the 20th century. The PVT invited us all to understand the development of our nervous system, the impact that our life experiences (traumatic or not) have on us, and how to cultivate tools to increase our vagal tone.

The PVT also expands our perspective of the nervous system; that is, instead of seeing it as a two-part system separated into the sympathetic antagonist and the parasympathetic protagonist, Dr. Porges identified a third type of nervous system response—the social engagement system—and offered us a hierarchical perspective based on whole-self integration and safety. The social engagement system picks up signals from people in our environment, including body language and facial expressions. Depending on what we see, we might experience either a relaxation response or a fight-or-flight response. The social engagement system has the power to override stress hormones if we receive soothing cues from our external environment, such as beautiful soft music or the kindness of a stranger. This can release oxytocin, a hormone that influences experiences of empathy and generosity.

Interestingly, because we are influenced on an unconscious level by the social engagement system, we know the least about it in comparison to the parasympathetic and sympathetic systems. However, it is powerful when it comes to regulating our emotions and preventing the release of cortisol. At the same time, the way our social engagement system works is often connected to powerful experiences we had in our developmental years. That is, if we grew up in a chaotic or anxiety-inducing home, it's likely that we didn't build valuable links that enable us to soothe ourselves and to self-regulate intense emotions like anxiety. Thus, even a welcoming face—which might normally cue our social engagement system to release oxytocin and calm us down—might be construed as a threat. Based on these early experiences, it could be useful to engage in activities that help tone the vagus nerve, and to also consult a specialist who works with trauma.

It's possible to tone the vagus nerve through a number of relaxation techniques including deep and slow belly breathing, immersing the face in cold water after vigorous exercise, loud singing, and submerging the tongue in a mouth filled with saliva, which can trigger the relaxation response.

Ideally, however we respond to a stressful situation, we will be doing so through what is known as the *window of tolerance*. This term describes the zone in which we can function most effectively and in which we can readily integrate information and respond to the demands and difficulties of our daily lives. Practices that help us tone the vagus nerve also help us expand our window of tolerance.

Fight　　Flight

HYPERAROUSAL
Rajas energy
Sympathetic Nervous System

movement toward　　　　*movement away*
anger　　　　　　　　　　　panic
rage　　　　　　　　　　　　fear
irritation　　　　　　　　　anxiety

Window of Tolerance

REGULATION
Sattva energy
Parasympathetic Nervous System (Ventral Vagal)

awareness/engagement
curiosity
compassion
patience

Freeze

HYPOAROUSAL
Tamas energy
Parasympathetic Nervous System (Dorsal Vagal)

immobility/shut-down
hopelessness
depression
disassociation

Proprioception, Interoception, and Neuroception

The internal workings of our inner technology are mysterious to many of us, and not commonly talked about in most circles. But I want to introduce you to three important terms in neuroscience that correspond to our somatic experience; they are *proprioception*, *interoception*, and *neuroception*.

In 1906, Sir Charles Sherrington published a landmark work called *The Integrative Action of the Nervous System*, in which he coined the term *proprioception*. Proprioception is mediated by proprioceptors, or mechanosensory neurons located within muscles, tendons, and joints. It helps us orient ourselves and move safely through space. Essentially, proprioception gives us an awareness of where our body is in space. It also contributes to things like coordination, body awareness, posture, speech, focus, and self-regulation.

Many things can impair our proprioception, including viruses, illnesses, amputations, and trauma. Through our proprioceptors, we are able to understand our optimal range of motion, our edges, and how to find the balancing point between stillness and activity. Yoga postures and movements are excellent for developing proprioception—especially hatha yoga practices, which invite flow and the ability to hold forms to explore and develop muscular integration.

It is very easy to utilize yoga to develop proprioception, but yoga's original intent helps us to develop the kind of safety we need so that we can move inward toward more subtle aspects of our inner technology.

In the same 1906 paper by Sherrington, he also coined the term *interoception*. Interoceptors are located mainly inside your organs, including your skin. These receptors carry information from the body to the brain. Interception invites you to assess what is happening *inside* the body. These assessments might include how you are feeling; whether you need to breathe more deeply; whether you need to use the bathroom; and whether you are hungry, cold, full, hot, itchy, etc. A developed interoceptive system aids in self-awareness, problem-solving, social understanding, flexible thinking, intuition, and emotional recognition.

Interoception is the system in which we explore the emotional dimension. Through it, you can ascertain whether you are feeling nervous, sad, happy, peaceful, content, scared, and a range of other emotions.

Thoughtful breathwork that invites you to become present has been shown to further develop the skill of interoceptive attunement. Why is this important? Because if you don't know how to check in, how will you know what you need?

Breathing is a powerful way to develop interoception. In addition, learning to map and label our feelings and to associate them with sensations and levels of intensity can offer us the internal vocabulary we need in order to be connected to our innermost feelings.

Finally, we come to neuroception. A term coined by Stephen Porges in 1984, *neuroception* is an unconscious system that assesses safety. Porges defines neuroception as a "process through which the nervous system evaluates risk without requiring awareness. This automatic process involves brain areas that evaluate cues of safety, danger and life threat…Neuroception is not always accurate. Faulty neuroception might detect risk when there is no risk or identify cues of safety where there is risk."

Neuroception of safety is necessary before social engagement can occur. This sense of safety relies on our ability to proprioceptively and interoceptively feel intact and connected.

The practices offered in the whole-self-care-plan section attune us proprioceptively and interoceptively, which helps cultivate a greater sense of safety so that we can respond rather than blindly react to life. Because our sensory system is managed by our subconscious and impacted by our past experiences, this is good news—it demonstrates that neuroception can gradually change over time.

The eternal lotus
unfolding its center petals

Eight petals
within each a gem
each gem worthy of its own investigation

Yet the more I looked into each one
I saw myself clearer and clearer
until I became the eternal blossoming lotus

Chapter Five:

A Whole-Self-Care Plan

"Seek to be whole, not perfect."
Oprah Winfrey

After years of working with individuals, I have come to understand that it really doesn't take much to make a shift. The hardest part for people is finding the discipline.

You cannot imagine how hard it is for many people to consistently be able to maintain a daily home practice. In a recent social media post, I asked what keeps people from practicing their yoga self-care. One practitioner mentioned the dreaded *D* word, discipline.

For years, as a teacher, I have been trying to understand the secret turn-on switch to get someone to show up for themselves. What motivates someone to be disciplined enough to include the use of more subtle practices, simple movement, breathwork, and contemplation? I have learned that it is different for each person. The nuances of our individual life experiences impact our relationship with ourselves and our habits. The story of our lives impacts our relationship to discipline. So much discipline has been instilled through fear. Today, we understand that these tactics have backfired.

We wander from discipline with no firm ground. We do not have an intimate relationship with our deep, calm center, which is naturally pulsating with the essence of life: peace, love, and compassion.

I approach discipline as an act of devotion. It seems that in life, we can easily be slaves to discipline, but can we be devotees who commit to practices from love rather than obligation?

Thankfully, it's possible to shift our habits of violation into habits of whole-self-care and rigorous devotion to what is precious.

I believe transforming our chores into rituals that we consciously choose is a transformational step in evolving from a slave mentality into a devotional one. Sadly, for many, only when our stress or suffering reaches unbearable levels does this inquiry begin (or is forced to happen).

If you have the gift of being able to wake up, then you have the responsibility to take care of the gift you've been given.

Who gave you the gift? No one knows, but many have a sense. Many have even defined it, but it remains part of the great mystery. I have a sense of how the grace of life enters me, but I don't know what is making my heart continue to beat and my breath to flow into this new day. This not-knowing keeps my heart humble. All I know is, *Wow, I made it to another day.*

I have experienced many days, even years, when I wondered what life was all about. In moments of loneliness and depression, I have questioned whether or not I need to even participate in this life. However, I kept my focus on the fact that I awakened that morning and there must be a reason for it. I may not know it, but I can simply wish for the day ahead to reveal to me what I need to know.

During a recent immersion, my teachers, the Mohans, shared the wisdom of *ishvara*. In Yoga, *ishvara* is an eternal friend that is within all of us. It is not a creator God. It is an aspect of ourselves that inspires us. In short, our individual consciousness that searches for eternal consciousness.

I am only sharing this to set up the ultimate sense of connection to the divine as the entire objective of yoga and the ultimate reason to practice whole-self-care. However, let's begin with what is possible today. Let's begin with first showing up for yourself every day, gathering your breath, mind, and body into a state of peace. The Mohans always say, "Know what is the ultimate, and achieve what is possible."

The whole-self-care practices in this section are offered with these parameters for safety:

- **Choose your practices:** Choose morning, afternoon or evening; you can do all three practices, or start by doing one daily. Perhaps one day you will wish to do a morning practice, and the next day, due to your household schedule, you will choose to do an evening practice.
- **Proprioception and interoception:** Cultivating these skills is part of every suggested routine, especially in order to develop your neuroceptive system and cultivate a sense of safety. However, you might choose to do a more physical, proprioceptive practice in the morning and a more emotional/mental, interoceptive practice in the evening.
- **Show up as you are:** You do not need a yoga mat or special clothing for any of these practices, which are

designed to be done wherever you are and under any circumstances.

- **Support is available:** If you have purchased this book, it comes with a free 30-minute consultation. It's yours, so use it if you like! Sign up at www.maryamovissi.com. You can also find detailed videos for some of the rituals in this section at www.maryamovissi.com/whole-self-care-rituals.

Whole-Self-Care: Morning Rituals

Acknowledge, Rise, and Breathe

Imagine that when the sun rose, you could hear its crackling waves of power fill the air and sky. Some animals get to experience the morning this way. As humans, we have been gifted with beautiful thin coverings over the exposed parts our brain: our eyes. Our eyelids have been perfectly designed. Just enough thickness can detect the shift of darkness to light. The eye's dance up and down is called a blink; this unique movement bathes the eye in oil and mucus, keeping it moist. Just like the breath, we can exercise some voluntary control over our eyes. We can have stare-offs with friends. And we can blink our eyes shut when we choose not to see something that may be disturbing or when we are anticipating a surprise.

If some of you experience sight impairment, it is still important to pay attention to the muscles around the eyes. However, what stimulates you to wake up might be sound.

The morning is invited into the body first through the perception of light through our eyes. Now, what happens when we don't have any sunlight around us? Most likely, an alarm will be what wakes up. Whatever it is, at some point, you will need to open your eyes and/or ears.

When we open our eyes/ears, we are often still lying in bed. We usually take a few moments to check our surroundings, and the mind starts churning. With the day ahead, so much can start to flow through the field of the mind. We can let the mind just run, or we can take a conscious pause and acknowledge our arrival in the new day.

You can do all the following practices, or just start with the first one and add a new practice into your routine each week. All three practices in total take 10 to 15 minutes.

Morning Ritual #1: Acknowledge

While you are still in bed:
- Open your eyes/ears and gently scan the room.
- Invite a sense of appreciation for this moment of opening your eyes and being alive and present. If this is hard to do, place a little note somewhere close by that you can see when you wake up. It should simply say, "What can I be grateful for in this moment?" If you are sight-impaired, choose a song or listen to the sounds that invite this feeling.
- Practice this for three weeks, and it will become second nature.

When you are out of bed:
- Locate a space where you are comfortable, be it a chair, couch, or floor pillow.
- Find a nature-based object that you can gently gaze at or perhaps hold in your hand: a plant, flower, water, stone, crystal, etc.
- Place the object in your hand and begin to soften your gaze on it.

- Become aware of your breath; follow the breath as it moves into your body. Pause, and observe how it leaves your body. Pause again; repeat this process for one to three minutes.

The tradition of greeting the morning is ancient and profound. When we begin our day with a humble heart, awakened body, and connection to our breath, we travel differently through our day. The out-of-bed contemplation invites us to connect to our sensual dimension through intimacy with nature.

When we slow down rather than pop out of bed and rush around just to get into our cars, trains, and buses, we navigate differently. These days, we're experiencing more stress-related diseases in the U.S. than ever before. If we do not gently break our cycle of rush, rush, rush, we will pay a price. Why not take a few minutes to arrive to the day integrated? This is probably the most important question to ponder right now.

Morning Ritual #2: Rise ~ Seven Movements of the Spine

Anatomist Gil Hedley has a powerful video called *The Fuzz Speech*. I often share this with clients and in classes, and I see transformations happen immediately. They become unbelievably clear and committed to one idea: *We are designed to move—and if we don't, we are in trouble!*

We wake up stiff, as though our body is trying to communicate to us. At first, it seems to whisper to us, "Please, please move me. Can't you feel I am stiff?" Sometimes, the voice gets louder and demands, "Don't you want to alleviate this tension and tightness?"

How often have you ignored this voice? Maybe one day, you wake up and experience your lower back in such a bind that your body doesn't whisper anymore—it shouts because it desperately wants you to hear.

Can we be more awake so we can hear the graceful whispers from our body and tune into the subtle signs it gives us? I believe we have an incredible capacity to hear them and just need to be tuned in. So let's tune in by creating a ritual of movement in the morning.

The spine moves in seven directions: forward, back, to the right and left, rotated in either direction, and lengthened. The routine, which you will find at <u>maryamovissi.com/whole-self-care-rituals</u>, will lead to more spinal flexibility.

The 7 Movements of the Spine

Elongation

Begin standing, feet about hip's width apart. Ground down through the feet and legs, as the spine grows tall through the crown of the head. Inhale to raise the arms up, reaching long through fingertips and staying grounded in the lower body. Exhale to bring hands back to heart center. Repeat twice.

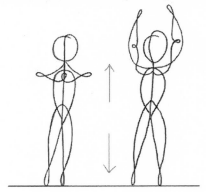

Lateral Bend - Left + Right

With arms reaching up, exhale to side bend to the left. Keep hips facing forward, opening up the right side of the body. Inhale back to center, exhale other side. Repeat twice, inhaling back to center in between each side.

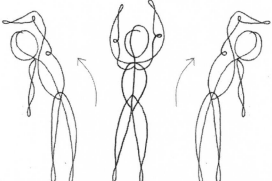

Spinal Rotation – Left + Right

Inhale to reach the arms up. Exhale to twist to the right, leading with the heart; arms lower to parallel the floor, right arm reaching back. Keep the collarbones wide, staying rooted through the legs. Inhale back to center. Repeat twice.

Flexion

Inhale to elongate the spine, reaching arms up. Exhale to fold over the legs, keeping knees bent to protect your hamstrings. You may enjoy staying here for a few breaths, gently rocking side to side.

Extension

From your forward fold, inhale to press palms into thighs, lengthening the spine. Collarbones wide, reach forward through the heart while sit bones reach back & up in a little backbend. Exhale to round the spine (flexion). Repeat three times.

Morning Ritual #3: Breathe: Got 90 Seconds?

Whether you do this after Ritual #1, while lying in bed, or after the movements of Ritual #2, that is your decision. You can even do it while you are making your breakfast. This practice takes about 90 seconds!

So we have gathered our mind and focused it on a sense of appreciation for the moment. Then we paid attention to body that allows us to "do" life. Finally, we arrive to the subtle realm: breathwork.

I believe everyone on the planet needs to obtain basic information about the breath. Here it is:

Your breath is voluntary and involuntary. Everything depends on your breath. The diaphragm is the prime muscle of the respiratory system. When we inhale, the diaphragm expands down and out. When we exhale, the diaphragm relaxes in and up.

The breath is your main tool for stress management. It's going to carry you through your day. It's going to help you navigate the ups and downs. No matter what, your breath will be with you. So why not develop an intimate relationship with your greatest companion? This companion came with you into this world and will leave with you.

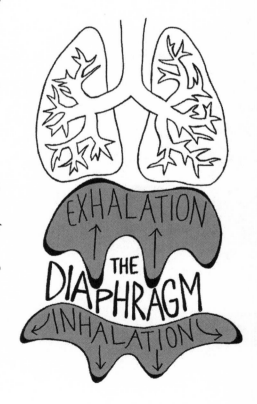

What a precious breath we have...let us hold it as such.

Begin by letting your hands rest on your lower ribs. Feel the shape change with each breath you take.

- Inhale; notice the sensation of expansion in your chest and ribs.
- Allow a natural pause.
- Exhale; notice the natural softening and movement inward of the diaphragm, and the sensation that complements it.
- Allow a natural pause.
- Repeat for about 90 seconds.

Having a daily breath practice is right up there with having a daily meditation practice. These two essential components of living a conscious life are great companions. The Bhagavad Gita states that the mind is like the wind: hard to tame. So instead of starting with the mind, let's start with the breath and invite the mind to follow.

Whole-Self-Care: Afternoon Rituals

Pause, Reflect, and Rest

I recognize that mornings may not be ideal for everyone. I remember when my children were younger and I couldn't just wake up at 4 a.m. I simply practiced the in-bed gratitude routine and saved the more active self-care routines for when my kids were in school or for the afternoon. The reality is that life happens, and sometimes we need to pivot and make changes to our self-care based on the needs of the day. Whether morning, afternoon, or evening, make sure you set aside some time (5 to 15 minutes) every day to check in, versus check out!

Often, we hit a wall in the middle of the day, during which we are naturally called to pause. We have found ways to push past this, often with caffeine. Taking a pause in the middle of your day is essential. In this space, you can digest the learnings of the day and reflect on what is ahead. I find that so many people push through their days and end up in bed exhausted, only to wake up at 3 a.m. with the mind chatter going strong. Where is our ability to reflect and digest our day? Usually, by the evening, we are exhausted, so the afternoon is a perfect time to pause, reflect, and rest.

Afternoon Ritual #1: Pause

We can bring ourselves into the moment with this moving meditation mudra. We will utilize the lotus bud mudra, also known as *anjali*.

Hold the gesture that you see in the image, and then:

- Inhale and take the hands as wide as you are comfortable, watching the space open up in between your hands.
- Invite a gentle pause between breaths.
- Exhale, watch your hands come together, and pause.
- Repeat for six cycles, then close your eyes and continue for another four cycles.

Sometimes we don't realize how much we are processing. Pausing to enter the present moment essential for our ability to build the default mode network (DMN). The DMN is the aspect of the brain that integrates our experiences and activates when we check in. Taking a few minutes to breathe and be present is so good and wise for your brain, as you literally create space!

Afternoon Ritual #2: Reflect

You can use a journal or just sit and contemplate the day. Now do the following:

- Take two to four rounds of sun salutations (mat or chair version. You can find videos for both at www.maryamovissi.com/whole-self-care-rituals).
- Reflect on everything that has happened during the day.
- Notice what surprised you, what hurt you, and what made you smile.
- Make a choice as to what you want to extract as a lesson from the day.
- Affirm it for yourself: *Today, I learned* _____
- The other side of this is to ask yourself what negative thought or experience from the day has remained with you. You can affirm that by stating: *Today, I transform* _____

begin in
Mountain/Tadasana;
grounded, tall spine

inhale,
reach arms up
to the sky

inhale,
reach arms up
to the sky

exhale,
fold over
legs

exhale,
fold over
legs

Surya Namaskar
———
Sun Salutations

inhale,
halfway
lift

inhale,
halfway
lift

exhale,
reach hips
back & up to
downward dog

exhale,
plant hands,
step to plank;
inhale here

inhale,
lift from heart
up to low cobra

exhale,
bend elbows to
lower onto belly

I often have my clients do this activity with me weekly. Recently, a client came in to do yoga therapy for her Lyme's disease. I asked her about her week and inquired as to what she'd learned about herself and others. She responded immediately and in a sharp tone, "Absolutely nothing. I am so angry!"

I suggested that we do a few sun salutations and then talk about it. She agreed. We sat after two rounds, and she shared how it was her first week taking a very high dosage of antibiotics. I explained the relationship of her gut to brain and how these antibiotics can sometimes create a sense of ungroundedness because they affect our production of major neurotransmitters. She started to feel better and realized that this was why she couldn't pinpoint the reason, and it was making her even more angry.

After this discussion, she understood the compassion she needs to extend to herself as these intense levels of antibiotics enter her system. She ended the session by saying, "I transform my anger to compassion." This became the affirmation she said to herself throughout her journey with the antibiotics, and it was very effective. When I reached out the next day, she said the anger ceased in that single session, and it had been mitigated greatly with the tool I'd shared with her!

Afternoon Ritual #3: Rest

Many cultures observe the practice of the afternoon nap, which is an incredibly wise way of getting our necessary rest.

In *Why We Sleep*, author Matthew Walker states that we are not sleeping the way nature intended. Most of us are practicing a monophasic pattern of sleep: that is, one prolonged bout of about seven hours of sleep. Our nature requires biphasic sleep (two sleep cycles in a 24-hour cycle). In a study conducted by Harvard University, it was found that people who abandoned the afternoon nap had a 37% increased risk of death from heart disease. Walker states, "From a prescription written long ago in our ancestral genetic code, the practice of natural biphasic sleep, and a healthy diet, appear to be the keys to a long-sustained life."

Another fascinating study mentioned in an article titled "The Science of Naps" notes: "What's amazing is that in a 90-minute nap, you can get the same [learning] benefits as an eight-hour sleep period, and actually, the nap is having an additive benefit on top of a good night of sleep."

In another experiment, researchers found that an afternoon nap was about equal to a dose of caffeine for improving perceptual learning. But in other ways, a midday doze might trump your afternoon latte. People who napped performed better on a verbal word-recall task an hour after waking compared with people who took caffeine or a placebo. While caffeine enhances alertness and attention, naps boost those abilities in addition to enhancing some forms of memory consolidation.

Personally, I try to get home around 4 p.m. and take a 15-minute nap. I am always amazed at how refreshed I feel. Sometimes, the mind chatter is high, so I do a body scan and just quiet the mind and nervous system!

This ritual can be done lying down, with your legs up the wall, or in constructive rest on a chair or edge of a couch.

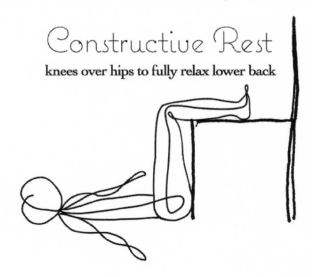

Constructive Rest
knees over hips to fully relax lower back

Body Scan Checklist

- Right foot, knee, leg
- Left foot, knee, leg
- Hips and lower back
- Middle and upper back
- Right shoulder, elbow, hand
- Left shoulder, elbow, hand
- Center of chest
- Neck
- Lower jaw
- Space between lips
- Space between eyebrows

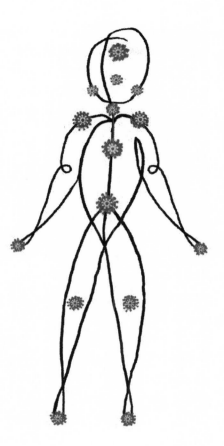

Let your brain rest in your skull as your body rests against the ground while you do this simple body scan. Notice how you feel afterwards.

Whole-Self-Care: Evening Rituals

Release, Massage, and Quiet

We are an extremely productive species. We can be driving to work, listening to an audiobook, and thinking about our day ahead all at once. Then, at our jobs, we might be juggling several tasks and several screens, and we might even skip lunch to get things done! Then we think about our households as we leave work to try to make it on time to pick up the dog or our children. It's a race against time as we rush over in order to avoid the $60 fine for being ten minutes late. Finally, we make it home—oh no, what about dinner!?

Needless to say, many of us enter the evening with our nervous system spent and on high alert.

give yourself sweet release

The evening rituals below are meant to bring balance to our day. You see, there is nothing wrong with a day like the one I mentioned above—it can be quite normal. It's what we do at the beginning and end of the day that often makes the greatest impact on our well-being.

Evening Ritual #1: Hip Release

I recommend that most people do a form of psoas release in the evening. The psoas, part of a pair of large muscles that run from the lumbar spine through the groin on either side of our body, is nestled deep in the trunk of the body. A little secret is that all things that are hidden deep in the cavities of the skull, ribcage, core, and hips are the keepers of your most central power. (This is a topic for my next book!)

The iliopsoas comprises the iliacus, a triangular muscle passing from the pelvis through the groin on either side, and the psoas. The iliopsoas helps to flex the hips.

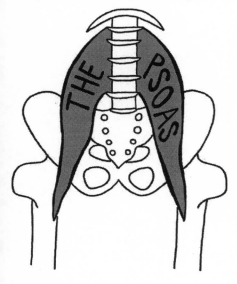

Although the release exercises I mention below will work on a majority of muscular networks in this region, I want to focus a bit on the psoas.

Remember the last time you hit the brakes really hard to avoid a major accident? The action originated in the psoas, which could still be gripping as a consequence of that action. I consider the psoas to be a keeper of our emotions. We often experience things that we just cannot say anything about. Sometimes we have flow with the "tribe" mentality and can't express ourselves out of a need for self-protection. A lot of those experiences are stored in the psoas and iliopsoas.

Dr. Christiane Northrup writes in one of her articles:

Your psoas muscles allow you to bend your hips and legs towards your chest, for example, when you are going upstairs. They also help to move your leg forward when you walk or run. Your psoas muscles are the muscles that flex your trunk forward when you bend over to pick up something from the floor. They also stabilize your trunk and spine during movement and sitting. The psoas muscles support your internal organs and work like hydraulic pumps allowing blood and lymph to be pushed in and out of your cells. Your psoas muscles are vital not only to your structural well-being, but also to your psychological well-being because of their connection to your breath.

You can probably surmise that the psoas needs your attention. The evening is a perfect time to do at least one psoas release practice. You can do both of the ones below or pick just one!

- A lunge (low lunge, for active psoas release)
- Reclined half happy baby (passive psoas release)

Low Lunge

Begin standing with a long spine and hands on your hips. Step one foot back, lowering your back knee onto your mat or a blanket. Let your hips sink toward the earth (finding more release in the psoas as you lower), staying strong & active in the legs. Maintaining a long spine, arms can reach up. Repeat on the opposite side.

Half Happy Baby

Start on your back with both legs in happy baby; release one leg and gently allow it to lengthen to the floor. Release & repeat on opposite side.

Evening Ritual #2: Massage

In the tradition of Ayurveda, a daily massage is an integral part of a self-care routine! In the U.S., we have the tradition of paying someone a lot of money to get bodywork and never learned some basic techniques that we can do every day.

First, before self-massage, start with quieting the senses. We are welcoming the wave of deep NREM (non-rapid-eye movement) sleep, or slow-wave sleep. Most of these deep waves are generated in the middle of your frontal lobes. One hour before sleep, it's important to quiet the room, decrease sensory distractions, and do the following:

- Lower light.
- Remove or obscure screens (phones, computers, TVs).
- Consider doing something repetitive and creative: knitting, drawing, playing music, listening to calming music for about 15 minutes, etc.
- Welcome yourself to the evening and to sleep.

Using your fingertips or thumbs, massage in the directions of the arrows as seen in the following diagrams. Begin with gentle pressure and use slow, fluid strokes, moving away from the center of the body or body part.

114

Ritual A: Feet Massage

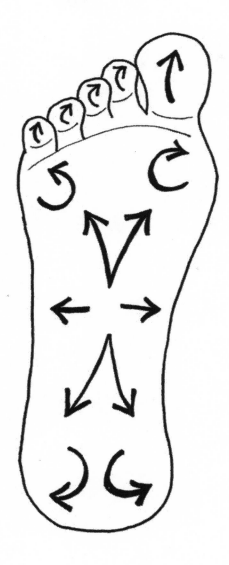

Ritual B: Forehead, Temples, Ears, Shoulders, Arms, and Hands Massage

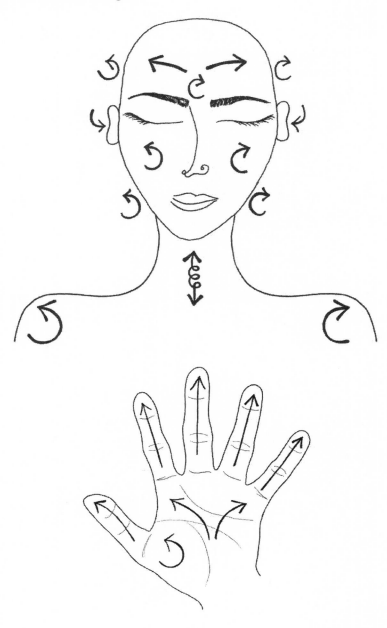

The specific areas targeted in the rituals above are also major gathering points of our fascia, a web that runs through the body. The fascia is a type of connective tissue that acts like a tensile webbing that keeps our entire body together, literally holding our tissues and organs in place. For hundreds of years, anatomists threw it out during dissections, regarding it as useless. Now we know it is the keeper of the whole self's well-being!

Evening Ritual #3: Quiet

This ritual is the thoughtful, systematic quieting of all our dimensions: body, mind, emotions, and energy. If you remember the gunas we discussed, we are inviting the qualities of tamas, which is what is needed for sleep and recovery.

The most effective tool to utilize at this time is the breath, and one of my favorites is left-nostril breathing, *chandra bhedana*. The translation of this Sanskrit term is "piercing the Moon," as the Moon represents calm, cool energy. Here's how to do a round of left-nostril breathing:

- Take a few rounds of a relaxed breath (longer exhale than inhale).
- Roll onto your right side if possible. You can also do this while sitting up in bed or lying face up.
- Close your right nostril with your index finger and begin to inhale through the left nostril. Exhale out of both nostrils, close the right nostril again with your index finger, and inhale through the left nostril. (If you know the half-valving methods, I highly encourage you to use them. I teach them in my webinar, *Rituals for Attuning to Your Nervous System During a Global Pandemic,* which you can find at www.maryamovissi.com/video) Then, breathe out of both nostrils. Keep repeating for at least two minutes.
- If this breath creates any agitation, kindly stop.

117

You might find that you fall asleep completely during this process or at least enter a relaxed state. The wisdom of this breath is based on the knowledge we have around the nostrils and valving. Every 90 minutes, we have a dominant nostril (go ahead—check it now). The body is literally regulating itself by naturally valving and changing the dominant nostril. The right nostril corresponds to our active, alert, and awakened states, and the left nostril to our calm, relaxed, creative states.

There is also right-nostril breathing, known as *surya bhedana* (piercing the Sun). The Sun represents dynamic, active energy. Sometimes, instead of your afternoon caffeinated drink, consider right-nostril breathing.

In yoga, we also use a breath practice called *nadi shodana* (energy channel clearing, also known as alternate-nostril breathing). This breath is used to open up both nostrils equally; although it can be very calming, it is also challenging and can be agitating without proper guidance. Alternate-nostril breathing is used to enter meditative states. I encourage you to learn this breath with a teacher.

A Support System for You!

I live and work in a place surrounded by yoga teachers and yoga therapists who embody what they teach. Therefore, they inspire the practitioners not only with their teachings but with their presence.

Let's return to Stephen Porges and his polyvgal theory. In his writing about social engagement and safety, he mentions how essential social bonding is for healthy human attachment. We now know more than ever that we need each other. We help inspire, motivate, and uplift one another. The opposite is also absolutely true.

118

There is a Sanskrit term called *sangha*. It refers to a community of like-minded people, a type of assembly and fellowship. In our journey through the care of the whole self, we must first make an individual choice. The choice is maintained through community support and being able to have a support system in the form of a sangha.

If you are reading this book and committed to the care of your whole self, then I want to offer you support. You will receive a 30-minute consultation with a Beloved Yoga teacher. We extend our sangha to support you. Why? Because I know we are on a trajectory of destruction in the United States. We have unprecedented levels of stress, dis-ease, cancer, psychological suffering, and pain that we need not succumb to. We live in an exceptional, uniquely beautiful world. Our species is part of an entire living ecosystem whose wisdom we can learn to tap into— especially if we attune to the inner technology of yoga, which has the power to complement our extraordinary external technology and offer solutions that are currently elusive on our planet.

Perhaps you want to find a community of like-minded people. First. join our online community and find a Care of the Whole Self Circle near you! Otherwise, I encourage you to find a nearby yoga studio that offers yoga and yoga therapy. Look for teachers that are 500-Hour Registered Yoga Teachers through the Yoga Alliance (YA) website or Yoga Therapists registered through the International Association of Yoga Therapists (IAYT).

Conclusion

After spending almost two decades in the field working with individuals who seek peace, not just in one aspect of themselves but in their whole self, I know that a person has to first make the choice and then find essential support in maintaining that choice.

May this book offer you wisdom to inspire your choice to take care of your whole self as well, and find the support you need and deserve.

In yoga, we have a saying: *Pade pade.* It means "step by step." I know we want things to change immediately. We live in a world where instant gratification is the new norm. However, sustainable change is slow, steady, impactful, and long-lasting.

Below is a tool I often use with my clients, and I offer it to you to use for your special journey through whole-self-care.

Lifestyle Habits

- Nourishment (diet)
- Relationships
- Daily routine

Movement

- Morning practice
- Afternoon practice
- Evening practice

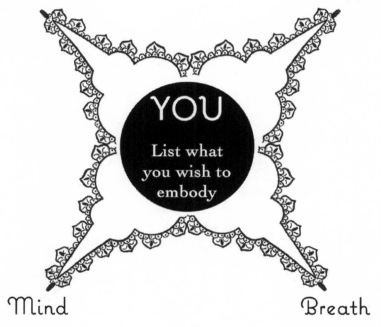

YOU

List what
you wish to
embody

Mind

- Concentration practice #1
- Concentration practice #2
- Meditation

Breath

- Daily breath practice
- Breath/Affirmation
- Breathwork for imbalance

I truly want you to take care of yourself—and if you integrate even one new habit you've found here with greater care, kindness, compassion, and love, then I've done my job.

The following *slokah*, or devotional hymn, is used in many rituals. It's a reminder that what we wish for ourselves is the same wish we desire for everyone.

Lokah samastha sukhino bhavantu
Om shanti shanti shantihi

May the world dwell in peace
May I dwell in peace
May you dwell in peace
May we dwell in peace
Peace (for the world)
Peace (for the community/country)
Peace (for you and your families)

Om…to the primordial hum we all return

Made in the USA
Middletown, DE
21 June 2021